The Teaching for Social Justice Series

William Ayers—Series Editor
Therese Quinn—Associate Series Editor

Girl Time: Literacy, Justice,
and the School-to-Prison Pipeline
MAISHA T. WINN

Grow Your Own Teachers:
Grassroots Change for Teacher Education
ELIZABETH A. SKINNER,
MARIA TERESA GARRETÓN, AND
BRIAN D. SCHULTZ, EDITORS

Holler If You Hear Me: The Education of a
Teacher and His Students, Second Edition
GREGORY MICHIE

Controversies in the Classroom:
A Radical Teacher Reader
JOSEPH ENTIN, ROBERT C. ROSEN, AND
LEONARD VOGT, EDITORS

Spectacular Things Happen Along the Way:
Lessons from an Urban Classroom
BRIAN D. SCHULTZ

The Seduction of Common Sense: How the Right
Has Framed the Debate on America's Schools
KEVIN K. KUMASHIRO

Teach Freedom: Education for Liberation
in the African-American Tradition
CHARLES M. PAYNE AND
CAROL SILLS STRICKLAND, EDITORS

Social Studies for Social Justice: Teaching
Strategies for the Elementary Classroom
RAHIMA C. WADE

Pledging Allegiance:
The Politics of Patriotism in America's Schools
JOEL WESTHEIMER, EDITOR

See You When We Get There:
Teaching for Change in Urban Schools
GREGORY MICHIE

Echoes of Brown: Youth Documenting
and Performing the Legacy of
Brown v. Board of Education
MICHELLE FINE

Writing in the Asylum: Student Poets in City Schools
JENNIFER MCCORMICK

Teaching the Personal and the Political:
Essays on Hope and Justice
WILLIAM AYERS

Teaching Science for Social Justice
ANGELA CALABRESE BARTON, with
JASON L. ERMER, TANAHIA A. BURKETT,
and MARGERY D. OSBORNE

Putting the Children First:
The Changing Face of Newark's Public Schools
JONATHAN G. SILIN AND CAROL LIPPMAN, EDITORS

Refusing Racism:
White Allies and the Struggle for Civil Rights
CYNTHIA STOKES BROWN

A School of Our Own: Parents, Power, and
Community at the East Harlem Block Schools
TOM RODERICK

The White Architects of Black Education:
Ideology and Power in America, 1865–1954
WILLIAM WATKINS

The Public Assault on America's Children:
Poverty, Violence, and Juvenile Injustice
VALERIE POLAKOW, Editor

Construction Sites: Excavating Race, Class, and
Gender Among Urban Youths
LOIS WEIS and MICHELLE FINE, Editors

Walking the Color Line:
The Art and Practice of Anti-Racist Teaching
MARK PERRY

A Simple Justice: The Challenge of Small Schools
WILLIAM AYERS, MICHAEL KLONSKY, and
GABRIELLE H. LYON, Editors

Teaching for Social Justice:
A Democracy and Education Reader
WILLIAM AYERS, JEAN ANN HUNT, AND
THERESE QUINN

Girl Time

Literacy, Justice, and the School-to-Prison Pipeline

Maisha T. Winn

Foreword by Shirley Brice Heath
Afterword by Michelle Fine

Teachers College
Columbia University
New York and London

Published by Teachers College Press, 1234 Amsterdam Avenue, New York, NY 10027

Photos by Kent D. Johnson, *Atlanta Journal-Constitution*

Library of Congress Cataloging-in-Publication Data

Winn, Maisha T.
    Girl Time : literacy, justice, and the school-to-prison pipeline / Maisha T.
    Winn ; foreword by Shirley Brice Heath ; afterword by Michelle Fine.
       p. cm. — (The teaching for social justice series)
    Includes bibliographical references and index.
    ISBN 978-0-8077-5200-5 (pbk. : alk. paper)
    ISBN 978-0-8077-5201-2 (hardcover : alk. paper)
       1. Girl Time (Program) 2. Prison theater—United States. 3. Women
    prisoners—Education—United States. 4. Women prisoners—Recreation—
    United States. 5. Critical pedagogy—United States. I. Title.
    HV8861.W56   2011
    365'.668—dc22   2010049624

ISBN 978-0-8077-5200-5 (paper)
ISBN 978-0-8077-5201-2 (hardcover)

Printed on acid-free paper
Manufactured in the United States of America

18   17   16   15   14   13   12   11   8   7   6   5   4   3   2   1

For all my girls!

We write to expose the unexposed. If there is one door in the castle you have been told not to go through, you must.

—Anne Lamott

Program

Series Foreword   ix

Curtain Speech, by Shirley Brice Heath   xiii

Acknowledgments   xviii

Dismantling the Single Story: A Prologue   1

      Learning the Ropes: A Double-Dutch Methodology   8

      Kemba's Nightmare/My Nightmare   10

      Traversing the Terrain   11

Act I.   **"Voices Can Be Heard":**
        Theatre for Incarcerated Girls   15

      Warming Up with Girl Time   21

      "We All Have a Past": Staged Readings   23

      Building Sandcastles: The Road to Writing   25

      Speaking Up and Talking Back: Actors and "Spectactors"   27

      The Journey Toward "Home"   29

Act II.   **"Yes, and":**
        Teaching Freedom in Confined Spaces   31

      Daring to Teach   34

      "A House Where You Are Called": Kaya   35

      "Completely Unqualified and Immensely Responsible": Anne   42

      "Little Black Girl": Zaire   44

      "As Long as I Wasn't the Star": Carrie Mae   47

      "Standing for What's Best in Them": Petulia   49

      "Theatre Is What Held It Together for Me": Isis   52

      "I Was the Identifier": Mindy   55

      "Drama Brat": Ginger   57

      "Theatre Is Like a Free Thing": Julisa   62

      Teaching for Social Justice   65

Act III.   "We Try to Find Our Way Home":
           Formerly Incarcerated Girls Speak   67

           "I Came Back to Deliver a Message": Nia   73
           "Where I Can Feel Free All the Time": Sanaa   81
           "Kinda Proving Myself": Jada   91
           "Real Girls Can Do This": Lisa   97
           "I Just Want to See Everything": Janelle   101
           Discussion   105

Act IV.   The Trouble with Black Girls: Racing, Classing,
           and Gendering the School-to-Prison Pipeline   107

           The Road to Good Character or Another Dead End?   110
           Sugar and Spice: The Remix   113
           The Trouble with Black Girls   117
           Rewriting the Script   120

Act V.   Magic Carpets and Fairylands:
           Preparing for a Performance of Possibilities   121

           Girl Power (Not Just Programs)   123
           Planting the Seeds of Participation   126
           Learning from Student Artists   132
           Learning from Teaching Artists   140
           Some Final Thoughts   143

Talk-Back/Talk-With:
           How Does One Applaud in Text? by Michelle Fine   145

           Freedom   146
           Commitment   149

Appendix A: "Ghosts of the Past" Script   153

Appendix B: "Beauty and the Thug" Script   155

Appendix C: "Ride or Die" Script   158

Notes   161

References   163

Index   169

About the Author   174

Series Foreword

Schools serve society; society is reflected in its schools. Schools are in fact microcosms of the societies in which they're embedded, and every school is both mirror of and window into a specific social order. If one understands the schools, one can see the whole of society; if one fully grasps the intricacies of society, one will know something about how its schools must be organized.

In a totalitarian society schools are built for obedience and conformity; in a kingdom, schools necessarily teach fealty and loyalty to the crown; under apartheid, educational privileges and oppressions are distributed along the color line. These schools might be "excellent" by some measures, but whatever else is taught—math or music, literature or science— the insistent curriculum under all else is the big lesson of how to function here and now: German schools in the middle of the 20th century produced excellent scientists and athletes and artists and intellectuals, and they also produced obedience and conformity, moral blindness and easy agreement, obtuse patriotism and a willingness to give orders that led to furnaces.

In an authentic democracy schools would aim for something entirely different: a commitment to free inquiry, questioning, and participation; a push for access and equity and simple fairness; a curriculum that encouraged independent thought and judgment; a standard of full recognition of the humanity of each individual. In other words, schools in a vibrant democracy would put the highest priority on the creation of free people geared toward enlightenment and liberation.

When the aim of education is the absorption of facts, learning becomes exclusively and exhaustively selfish, and there is no obvious social motive for learning. The measure of success is always a competitive one— it's about comparing results and sorting people into winners and losers. People are turned against one another, and every difference becomes a potential deficit. Getting ahead of others is the primary goal in such places, and mutual assistance, which can be so natural, is severely restricted or banned. On the other hand, where active work is the order of the day, helping others is not a form of charity, something that impoverishes both recipient and benefactor. Rather a spirit of open communication, interchange and analysis becomes commonplace, and there's a recognition that the people you're trying to help know better. Of course in these places, there is a certain natural disorder, a certain amount of anarchy and chaos as there is in any busy workshop. But there is a deeper discipline at work, the discipline of getting things done and learning through life, and there is an appreciation of knowledge as an inherently public good—something that can be reproduced at little or no cost, and unlike commodities, when it is given away, no one has any less of it. In a flourishing democracy, knowledge would be shared without any reservation or restrictions whatsoever.

The education we're accustomed to is simply a caricature—it's neither authentically nor primarily about full human development. Why for example is education thought of as only kindergarten through 12th grade, or kindergarten through university? Why does education occur only early in life? Why is there a point in our lives when we no longer think we need education? Why again, is there a hierarchy of teacher over students? Why are there grades and grade levels? Why does attendance matter? Why is punctuality valuable? Why indeed, do we think of a productive and a service sector in our society, with education designated as a service activity? Why is education separate from production?

The development of free people in a free society—this is the central goal of teaching for social justice. This means teaching toward freedom and democracy, and it's based on a common faith in the incalculable value of every human being; it assumes that the fullest development of all is the condition for the full development of each, and conversely that the fullest development of each is the condition for the full development of all. One traditional way of expressing this ideal is this: whatever the wisest and most privileged parents in a democracy want for their kids becomes the standard for what we as a community want for all of our children.

The democratic ideal has policy implications, of course, but is deeply implicated as well in questions of teaching and curriculum. We expect schools in a democratic society to be defined by a spirit of cooperation, inclusion, and full participation, places that honor diversity while building unity. Schools in a democracy resist the overspecialization of human activity, the separation of the intellectual from the manual, the head from the hand and the heart from the brain, the creative and the functional. The standard is fluidity of function, the variation of work and capacity, the mobilization of intelligence and creativity and initiative and work in all directions.

While many of us long for teaching as something transcendent and powerful and free, we find ourselves too often locked in situations that reduce teaching to a kind of glorified clerking, passing along a curriculum of received wisdom and predigested bits of information. A fundamental choice and challenge for teachers, then, is this: to acquiesce to the machinery of control, or to take a stand with our students in a search for meaning and a journey of transformation. To teach obedience and conformity, or to teach its polar opposite: initiative and imagination, curiosity and questioning, the capacity to name the world, to identify the obstacles to your full humanity, and the courage to act upon whatever the known demands. On the side of a liberating and humanizing education is a pedagogy of questioning, an approach that opens rather than closes the prosy process of thinking, comparing, reasoning, perspective-taking, and dialogue. It demands something upending and revolutionary from students and teachers alike: repudiate your place in the pecking order, it urges, remove that distorted, congenial mask of compliance. You must change.

A generous approach to teaching grounds itself in cherishing happiness, respecting reason, and—fundamentally—in honoring each human life as sacred and induplicable. Clarity about classrooms is not based on being able to answer every dilemma or challenge or conundrum that presents itself, but flows rather from seeing classroom life as a work-in-progress—contingent, dynamic, in-the-making, unfinished, always reaching for something more. The ethical core of teaching is about creating hope in students. Because the future is unknown, optimism is simply dreaming, pessimism merely a dreary turn of mind. Hopefulness, on the other hand, is a political and moral choice based on the fact that history is still in-the-making, each of us necessarily a work-in-progress, and the future entirely unknown and unknowable. Teaching for social justice provides images of possibility—it can all change!—and in that way rekindles hope.

A robust, humanistic education for today can draw on the diverse threads spun by our freedom-seeking foremothers and forefathers. We begin by embracing the importance of dialogue with one another, and dialogue, as well, with a rich and varied past and a dynamic, unfolding future. Dialogue is both the most hopeful and the most dangerous pedagogical practice, for in dialogue our own dogmas and certainties must be held in abeyance, must be subject to scrutiny, and there will be, to be sure, inevitable mistakes and misunderstandings. But the promise remains that if we unlock the wisdom in the room, if we face one another without masks and as the best we can be, we each might contribute a bit, and we each might learn something powerful and new.

The core lessons of a liberating education—an education for participation, engagement, and democracy—are these: each human being is unique and of incalculable value, and we each have a mind of our own; we are all works-in-progress swimming through a dynamic history in-the-making toward an uncertain and indeterminate shore; we can choose to join with others and act on our own judgments and in our own freedom; human enlightenment and liberation are always the result of thoughtful action.

There are a series of contradictions in these propositions that must somehow be embraced, and not fled from: a focus on changing oneself, and a focus on engagement and change within a community; a concern with the individual, and a concern with the group; the demands of self activity and self education, and the location of that self within the social surround. An emphasis on the needs and interests of each individual must become co-primary with faith in a kind of robust public that can and must be created. To be exclusively child centered, to the extent that the needs of the community are ignored or erased, is to develop a kind of fatalistic narcissism, or, too often, a performance of whiteness; to honor the group while ignoring the needs of the individual is to destroy any authentic possibility of freedom. The challenge is to somehow hold on to the spirit of the old saying, "I am because we are, and we are because I am."

Education is an arena of struggle as well as hope—struggle because it stirs in us the need to look at the world anew, to question what we have created, to wonder what is worthwhile for human beings to know and experience—and hope because we gesture toward the future, toward the impending, toward the coming of the new. Education is where we ask how we might engage, enlarge, and change our lives, and it is, then, where we confront our dreams and fight our notions of the good life, where we try to comprehend, apprehend, or possibly even transform the world. Education is contested space, a natural site of conflict—sometimes restrained, other times in full eruption—over questions of justice.

—William Ayers
Therese Quinn

Curtain Speech

Shirley Brice Heath

This book opens for readers a sense of what experience with dramatic arts can mean for young women incarcerated within the juvenile detention system. A theatre program gives these young women opportunities to experience theatre pieces written and performed by formerly incarcerated girls. In special events within youth detention centers, these formerly incarcerated girls perform their work and talk with their incarcerated peers about what they know and think about negotiating their future and putting their past in perspective.

This book raises tough issues about the redemptive power of short-term voluntary programs in the arts for young women trying to emerge from family and education systems that offer little in the way of emotional or cognitive support. Sociocultural activity theory and performance ethnography frame the book's depictions of ways in which the young women struggle to find their own identities and to reconcile what others may see in their past records with their own resolve for a different kind of life on the other side of their time within juvenile detention. Throughout this book, questions about the young women's struggles with their future intertwine with the doubts, fears, and need for persistent faith by the artist-educators who design and implement the program. These professionals hold out high hopes for the redemptive powers of the arts, but the course of interactions and any reciprocity of faith in renewal and "fresh chances" for formerly incarcerated young women do not always move forward smoothly.

Winn lays out to us how the girls perform and perceive the roles they play in the fictional dramatic pieces they weave from factual bits of the lives they have seen and lived. In doing so, Winn brings to mind theories of play and performance that rarely enter the professional preparation for teachers at the secondary level. How does saying the words of a character within a dramatic performance matter in the human psyche of the actor? How do mimicry, imitation, adaptation, and improvisation reflect the mind at work within the moment of being someone other than the self that will return when the curtain goes down? Finally, how can dramatic play build empathy for others and a sensitivity to when "difference" is most likely to "make a difference"?

In her play *Fires in the Mirror* (1993), actress and playwright Anna Deavere Smith turned herself into Jewish and Black males and females, young and old. She recounted in the introduction to this play how she grew as a young woman to realize that control over words—one's own and those of roles that actors play—can aid the search for character. She describes words as being in the body: "The act of speech is a physical act. It is powerful enough that it can *create*, with the rest of the body, a kind of cooperative dance. That dance is a sketch of something that is inside a person, and not fully revealed by the words alone" (pp. xxv–xxvi).

Smith's description, the current volume, and numerous studies of the arts echo the faith that art does make differences that matter. This conviction, taken in faith, has lived for decades within the hearts of humanists and educators with a humanistic bent. But the hard sciences have given little evidence to support this faith in cognitive benefits of short-term or long-term participation in the arts.

However, in recent years, cognitive neuroscience research has increased understanding of how the brain works within states of mind—empathy, visualization, embodiment, and imagination—that come with artistic endeavor. Though this work does not, nor will it ever, recommend cause-and-effect absolutes, artists and educators will do well to consider current findings that point to the merits of certain aspects of learning environments that inevitably arise from arts practice.

Foremost among these considerations should be the critical importance of sustaining participation in the arts. The majority of programs, such as that documented in the current volume, operate for only short durations. Funding is simply not available to sustain the existence of the arts—particularly for sidelined populations, such as youth in the juvenile justice system. Yet cognitive neuroscience research underscores the essential value in youth development for the sustained practice and envisionment of advancing skills that come only through longitudinal work. What happens when individuals *play* (e.g., practice through performance) roles other than those assigned to them by society members. Playing these roles means that individuals envision themselves to be other than what their circumstances have seemingly destined them to be—for example, troublemaker, loser, punk, prostitute, or criminal-in-the-making. Entering dramatic roles that call up a range of attitudes, uses of language, resources in bodily presentation, and emotional alignment enlists human capacities so often unseen by and unrealized for youth whose early socialization has sent messages and given models of negativity.

This volume offers several key provocations for educators. Foremost is the need for sensitivity to how the penal system figures in the lives of an increasing proportion of females—daughters, mothers, wives, and girlfriends—in the United States. Equally important is an awakening to the potential of dramatic arts for "serious" learning. So often, the arts are dismissed as "frivolous," "diversionary," or "recreational." Instead, the learning environment created with the arts—from dance to drama, from jazz ensembles to garage bands, from painting to film production—insists upon practices, linguistic and cognitive, that provide foundational support for *all* learning. Primary perhaps is the fact that commitment within the arts means looking for ways to make "it" work—whatever "it" may be. In the dramatic arts, the sense of together "we could" accelerates assessment of one's own *capacity* ("Can I do this?"), promotes consideration of *permission* ("Is it appropriate for me to play a role from a script my friend wrote about her life?"), and builds *obligation* ("The group needs me as this character"). In essence, consciousness and reasoned consideration of acts and consequences link together in the maturation of empathetic understanding that comes through dramatic arts.

This volume should speak to audiences beyond those whose challenges come through their professional identity as classroom teachers. Community artists, actors and directors in community theatres, and leaders of museums and youth centers will find reason here to think of new kinds of alliances they might make by extending possibilities in the dramatic arts to new audiences. These artists and community resources can offer young people across the spectrum of home backgrounds the chance to create worlds together, not just the world on the stage, but social worlds where the young can absorb what it means to choose, create, and critique collaboratively.

Acknowledgments

It is my husband, Lawrence T. Winn, who supported my research and writing with abundant love and grace. His work with incarcerated boys in Newark, New Jersey, helped me think critically about the intersection of race, class, and gender in the juvenile justice system. Lawrence's patience—especially on weekends when I was in my writing cave—and his encouragement when I was running out of steam, are unparalleled.

Obasi Rais Winn, my son and first-born child, was incredibly cooperative as I completed this manuscript. Obasi inspired me to get my manuscript completed so I could properly welcome him into this world without the worry of looming deadlines. Obasi is undoubtedly my best work yet. I thank him for his love and patience while I was hanging out with the girls!

Bill Ayers, Emily Renwick, and Carole Saltz rock! Bill was instrumental in helping me develop the prospectus for *Girl Time* and always available via cell—especially during road trips on open stretches of highway! Emily and Carole were vital in helping me process some of my ideas and supportive when I changed my mind about certain aspects of the manuscript.

I am deeply humbled by the ways in which Shirley Brice Heath and Michelle Fine engaged my work. Shirley has been hearing about this project for a long time and has offered great wisdom along the way. Michelle, a new colleague, jumped right on board bringing her passion, insight, and deep commitment to our young people.

I am deeply indebted to my undergraduate research assistant, Stephanie Spangler, who joined the project through the Emory University's Scholarly Inquiry and Research at Emory (SIRE) program. Stephanie brought her contagious enthusiasm, unwavering commitment, and became a tour de force on this project.

Additionally, I am grateful to the Emory University's Race and Difference Initiative and specifically a summer research grant for faculty that enabled me to hire a graduate student research assistant, Chelsea A. Jackson, for the project. Chelsea worked tirelessly on data management, transcriptions, assisting with exit interviews, and keeping me sane during the last months of writing. Chelsea is a budding scholar in her own right.

Dr. Susan Cridland-Hughes, Latrise Johnson, and Nadia Behizadeh extended their helping hands during various phases of the project. Susan assisted with filming during the summer 2008 program, and Latrise and Nadia were key in assembling materials for Girl Time teaching artists for the teacher training workshops.

I am so humbled by students in the Division of Educational Studies at Emory University such as those who attended Girl Time events through-out the past 4 years, including Keisha Green (who brought her students), Latrise Johnson (who brought her sister, Denise Johnson, and their moth-er), Michelle Purdy, Chelsea Jackson, Nadia Behizadeh, and Fahima Ife. I was also fortunate enough to have the support of colleagues along the way, including Dr. Jackie Jordan Irvine and Dr. Jennifer Gandhi, who both attended Girl Time events. Family and friends also became big fans of the Girl Time program, including Jill Marie Butler, Michael and Ratima Smith, my brother, Dr. Damany Fisher, and, of course, my husband, Lawrence T. Winn. As with all my work, my father, Dr. James A. Fisher, was a catalyst for debate and discussion, which inspired me to write with clarity and purpose.

I would not make it in the academy without my academic "BFF," Valerie F. Kinloch, and her endless support. No scholar should be without such a friend.

Rhodessa Jones has been an inspiration for this work. When I first learned of The Medea Project: Theater for Incarcerated Women, I was humbled and hungry to grapple with issues of incarceration for women and girls.

Last but never least, I must acknowledge the brilliant ensemble of women and girls with whom I worked for the last 4 years: Susie, Nyrobi, Brooklyn, Jamarah, Jennifer, Brenda, Theresa, Jeronique, Rachel, Heidi, Nia, Sanaa, Lisa, Jada, Janelle, and many others.

I am abundantly grateful to the very talented photojournalist, Kent Johnson, for allowing me to use his beautiful photographs throughout this book.

I would also like to acknowledge Teachers College Press for permis-sion to reproduce a small section of my chapter, which first appeared in Valerie F. Kinloch's (2011) *Urban Literacies: Critical Perspectives on Language, Learning, and Community*, in Act II.

Proceeds from *Girl Time* will go to Rhodessa Jones' The Medea Project: Theater for Incarcerated Women and to Synchronicity Perfor-mance Group's Playmaking for Girls program, both of which work with incarcerated women and teen girls respectively.

Dismantling the Single Story
A Prologue

"It all started when I was in elementary school. I was really poor. So I had all hand-me-downs and torn up clothes. And the other kids, they all looked nice and had nice clothes. They saw me and they wanted to pick on me. Even my brothers would say, 'That ain't my little sister, I don't know her.' And they used to judge me like that. And ever since then, I just feel like people don't like me and people judge me." (Rae)

"I am committed to the state. It's like 50 percent of me belongs to my mom and 50 percent of me belongs to the state. It's like if you had a bag of candy and half of it was actually yours but the other half belonged to someone else. I will be committed for eight years. But I am praying. I know I did bad and I'm going to do better." (Diamond)

"Since second grade, I've been in gifted school until I was in ninth. I was, from second to sixth, in the gifted music instrument orchestra type of school . . . So basically all my life I was doing singing and working with instruments." (Jill)

"I'm not using my past as a crutch, so I don't walk around trying to make pity party stories, and I know that regardless of what happened, and regardless of what people did to you, you still can make something out of yourself." (Jennifer)

"I know I get mad a lot, I don't know. I let small things irritate me. But I do write. And writing makes me feel very, very powerful. I think when I write I've conquered my fears or handled my situation in a very positive way. And me being able to act my writings out or my feelings out in a positive way, you know, is not negative. I'm just not having the attitude. I get to put myself in other characters. And it may be the character's feelings, but I'm also able to express my own feelings towards a similar situation or experience through the characters. And I think that's very good." (Sanaa)

"The reason I decided to go to the army was because if I stay out here I might get into some trouble or something I do not want to get into. I feel like it's going to be better for me as an independent person, as a daughter, as me being responsible." (Nia)

"A lot of people don't think that 14-year-olds and 13-year-old girls are out there prostituting and having pimps and getting pregnant. So it's like, we are gonna show people that these things really do happen and show people the full story . . . and that girls do kind of keep getting into trouble out there on the streets. But girls can change it all around. It's up to us if we want to change or not. Like you can't tell a person to change and they're gonna change. It has to be up to that person." (Jada)

"I went to jail because my mom used to put me out. She didn't like me. I looked too much like her, so she put me out and listed me as a runaway. And I went to jail but I got out a few weeks later . . . I ran away my second time . . . because [my mom] put me out and I tried to come back . . . but [my mom] was choking me. And I started coughing up blood so I hid in the back and I ran out and never came back. So she listed me as a runaway and I went to jail. I tried to tell the police, but they didn't care." (Candy)

"The reason I ended up in jail was because of arson. Sometimes I can get very, very angry, and when I do get angry the only thing that pops up in my mind is fire. And I'm interested in science to tell the truth." (Tichina)

"Well, the first time I got locked up was because . . . I wanted to be like my sister. I wanted to hang out with her and stuff. So my grandma works from 7 in the morning to 7 at night. So I would just go around with my sister and hang with her. So I basically stopped going to school. And then I had to go live with my momma. When they enrolled me in school, they seen in my record that I missed a whole semester. So then I only went one day and then I stopped going to school. I didn't go back and they locked me up for truancy." (Viola)

"Now I love to dance. I love children, but I don't want none at all. I love children. I mean there's nothing I can do without the children. I work in a daycare and I love them. They all love me. Every time they get off the bus, they come and see me. They hug me." (Taraji)

"I'm pregnant . . . and the dad is really happy. And I want to raise my child up to be a good son, you know, and I want him to do good things." (Lisa)

"[Performing] means a lot to me because it shows people that I am a lot more than meets the eye. You can't judge a book by its cover. Even though I was incarcerated, I still have my personality and my spunkiness. And I want to give that to other people." (Zoë)[1]

Led by a chorus of voices—the voices of formerly incarcerated girls—this prologue offers examples of the stories and experiences of girls who are living lives "betwixt and between" incarceration and freedom (Winn, 2010b). Girl Time, a theater program for incarcerated and formerly incarcerated girls in the urban southeast, uses playwriting and the power of theatre to unearth the multiple stories of incarcerated girls. Organized by a collective of women teaching artists including actors, directors, advocates of women's reproductive rights, youth workers, and people involved in a range of nonprofit organizations—Girl Time unapologetically focuses on issues impacting girls and women. Playwriting, in the context of Girl Time, embodies the need to listen to girls who have found themselves entangled in the juvenile justice system by inviting them to revisit, and in some cases rewrite, scenes from their lives, as well as the lives of their peers. By creating characters, developing dialogue, and seeking resolution in complex lives, formerly incarcerated girls who participate in Girl Time have an opportunity to reintroduce themselves through the medium of playwriting and performance.

When girls are released from Regional Youth Detention Centers (RYDCs) Girl Time invites them to participate in its summer program. The purpose of the summer program is to stage 8 to 10 plays, written by incarcerated girls in Girl Time RYDC workshops, and to create an ensemble that performs for the community in a public theater as well as for incarcerated youth in RYDCs. This multi-sited ethnography moves between institutions that jail youth and spaces that facilitate a discourse of second chances through a "performance of possibilities" (Madison, 2005). Therefore this study draws from data collected from working with formerly incarcerated girls—primarily African American and ages 14 to 17—who participated in Girl Time's intensive summer theatre program. In addition to analyzing the pedagogy of playwriting and performance in Girl Time

RYDC workshops over the course of three seasons (2006–2007, 2007–2008, and 2008–2009), I also synthesize the RYDC workshops with Girl Time's work beyond the confines of the detention centers.

Girl Time seeks to complicate the "single story" of girls who have found themselves in the school/prison nexus and the teachers who work with them. In her observations of the "danger of a single story," Nigerian novelist Chimamanda Adichie asserts that if you "show a people as only one thing . . . that is what they become."[2] Adichie's observations could easily be applied to the growing number of children who are being ushered from schools to prisons in what has been referred to as the *school-to-prison pipeline*. While boys still account for most arrests and subsequent detainment in youth detention centers, girls are increasingly being arrested and incarcerated (Chesney-Lind, 1999; Fine & McClelland, 2006; Polakow, 2000; Simkins, Hirsch, Horvat, & Moss, 2004). Belknap (2001) describes who are in girls' institutions:[3]

- On average, the girls are 14 to 15 years old.
- Many girls are poor and growing up in neighborhoods with high crime rates.
- 50% of the girls are African American, 34% are White, and 13% are Latino.
- Many girls have a history of poor academic performance and are sometimes pushed out of high school.
- Often the girls are victims of physical, sexual, and/or emotional abuse or exploitation.
- Girls sometimes have a history of using or abusing drugs and/or alcohol.
- Many girls have gone without medical and mental health needs being addressed.
- The girls feel that life is oppressive and lack any hope for the future.

Most recently, many girls have been accused of departing from the heteronormative trope of "sugar and spice" to the reputation of "no longer nice" (Prothrow-Stith & Spivak, 2006). Everything from music videos, single mothers, and girls going wild has been placed on trial and found guilty for the disappearance of childhood and innocence for particular girls. And while the importance of self-discipline (Yang, 2009) and personal responsibility are arguably important goals for all youth, individual choices and decisions are not the sole contributors to the school/prison nexus. A neoliberal movement to privatize what is largely a public failure to create a safety net for urban youth, and girls in particular, has convinced certain children that incarceration is to be expected as a reasonable part of their life cycle (Duncan, 2000; Fine & Ruglis, 2009).

In addition to examining the lives of incarcerated and formerly incarcerated girls, *Girl Time* also seeks to share the stories of educators who dare to teach children who have been "thrown away" (Bell, 2000). If education is political and if the educator is a politician, educators in the Girl Time teaching-artist ensemble operate from a platform that seeks "to know the concrete world in which their students' language, syntax, semantics, and accent are found in action, in which certain habits, likes, beliefs, fears, desires, are formed that are not necessarily easily accepted in the teachers' own worlds" (Freire, 2005, p. 129). To borrow from Freire, teaching artists in the Girl Time program are "cultural workers"—an idea I explore further in Act II. Girl Time teaching artists' purpose is to work with girls wherever they are along their learning journey and to co-construct a scaffold getting them from where they are to where they want to be. Playwriting and the act of bringing plays to life through performance is one of the most authentic ways for youth to represent their lives. Girls who have experienced isolation, abuse, and miseducation recast themselves while forging possible lives beyond labels and stereotypes. Perhaps even most importantly, teaching artists have the opportunity to really listen to and hear these girls' dreams and nightmares, and to experience the humility in realizing that the girls are the true teachers:

> Educators need to know what happens in the world of the children with whom they work. They need to know the universe of their dreams, the language [with] which they skillfully defend themselves from the aggressiveness of their world, what they know independently of schools, and how they know it. (Freire, 2005, p. 130)

Throughout this journey I examine the ways in which teaching artists and student artists—specifically incarcerated and formerly incarcerated girls—attempt to create freedom in confined spaces, as well as how they navigate marginalizing and oppressive institutions in order to cultivate and sustain educational, social, and personal freedom. Ultimately I argue that formerly incarcerated girls experience *liminality*, or "betwixt and between" lives, in which they can use playwriting and performance to try to find a way "home." Liminality, according to Madison (2005) is the "state of being neither here nor there—neither completely inside nor outside a given situation, structure, or mindset" (p. 158). Elsewhere I have examined the betwixt and between lives of formerly incarcerated girls through a lens that historicizes literacy and literate practices (Winn, 2010a and 2010b). More specifically, I adopted a framework drawing from studies of Black women speakers, writers, and "doers" of the word—not too far removed from slavery in the Americas and other forms of enslavement in the early 19th century (Peterson, 1995). Peterson argues that these women, or the "brave," who she examined "wrote from positions of marginality, from social, psychological, and geographic sites that were peripheral to the dominant culture and, very often to their own." (pp. 6–7). Much like Peterson, I find myself asking if formerly incarcerated girls can live lives beyond the single story of adjudicated youth and the images projected onto them by schools, communities, media, the public, and in some cases their families. Using Peterson's notion of liminality in the lives of Black women—who have experienced marginalization in various forms—I turn to her line of inquiry and ponder

> whether or not it is possible to imagine a scenario whereby the incarcerated could escape, and perhaps even return, the gaze of their wardens; undo the dominant culture's definitions of such binary oppositions as order/disorder, normal/abnormal, harmless/dangerous; break down those boundaries separating the one from the Other; and in the process create a space they could call home. (Peterson, 1995, p. 8)

In order to answer such a question, I journeyed through a Regional Youth Detention Center (RYDC, a multi-service center for children and youth who have been incarcerated); a public theatre that houses Our Place Theatre Company, the Girl Time program where formerly incarcerated girls learn about playwriting and theatre; and back to the RYDC, where formerly incarcerated girls return to perform plays and speak to their incarcerated peers. With one foot firmly planted in sociocultural activity theory (Engeström, 1999, 2001; Gutiérrez, Baquedano-López, & Tejeda, 1999; Nasir & Hand, 2006) and another foot planted in performance ethnography (Madison, 2005), I focus on the activities of playwriting and performance. Performance ethnography and, more specifically, Madison's notions of a "performance of possibilities" guide my work. Madison argues that a performance of possibilities "raises several questions for the ethnographer" (p. 172). Some of these questions that I explore in this work include:

- By what definable and material means will [formerly incarcerated girls] benefit from the performance?
- How can the performance contribute to a more enlightened and involved citizenship that will disturb systems and processes that limit freedoms and possibilities?
- In what ways will the performers probe questions of identity, representation, and fairness to enrich their own subjectivity, cultural politics, and art? (Madison, 2005, p. 172)

The Girl Time program is an ideal place to begin to question (and respond to) the ways in which girls experience being pushed out of schools and ushered through the school/prison nexus. Girl Time is also an important space to demonstrate the ways in which educators in out-of-school as well as in-school contexts can facilitate or co-facilitate learning in complicated contexts against the background of poverty and inadequate services for youth and their families. As educators align themselves with promoting social justice or teaching for social justice, this study questions whose justice and how can we ensure it for all youth? Girl Time will encourage the teaching for social justice discourse to include children who are behind bars moving through juvenile courts (Ayers, 1997) or who are being ushered from schools to jails. Girl Time's playwriting and performance pedagogy has much to offer social justice educators:

1. Girl Time teaching artists are coalition builders; that is, they are women involved in various organizations and practices committed to improving the lives of girls and women, and thus understand that the work of teaching for social justice cannot be done in silos.
2. Girl Time demonstrates how theatre, and specifically playwriting and performance, can serve as a meditational tool to negotiate lives that are between incarceration and freedom.
3. Girls Time, and the student artists in particular, offer insight into the racing, classing, and gendering of the school-to-prison pipeline.
4. Girl Time illuminates the critical role theatre can play in helping incarcerated and formerly incarcerated girls develop critical literacies through engaging in a performance of possibilities.

Learning the Ropes: A Double-Dutch Methodology

As a fellow teaching artist in the Girl Time program, I have been given the honor of trying to understand what it is we know about working with girls and how we know it, in order to support fellow educators in urban public schools as well as in teaching and learning communities beyond the classroom. Interviewing my co-teachers made me aware of my insider/outsider status. I was an "insider" because an ensemble of women invited me to share their journey as educators focused on working with girls who had been forgotten, neglected, and even reviled by many of the adults in their lives. I trained with Girl Time and became a teaching artist in their ensemble. My "outsider" status was obvious from my lack of theatre experience (okay, more like my nonexistent theatre background). Prior to working as a Girl Time teaching artist I had never worked with incarcerated youth and had only been in a youth detention center once in my life, on a "field trip." Additionally, I was an outsider to the southeast; I grew up in northern California and did not live in another state until I was 30 years old. Lastly, I was an outsider in that my experiences attending plays and performances were limited to being a passive audience member. Always a spectator, as opposed to Boal's notion of a "spectactor," I attended plays to be entertained, but never imagined how much responsibility I had to engage, make connections, and build bridges through the work. Through my study of Participatory Literacy Communities (PLCs), I learned how the role of the poet, author, performer, and audience blurred when words and language assumed a call to action (Fisher, 2003, 2004, 2006, 2007).

In a study of a youth collective engaged in the critical literacy practice referred to as "air shifting"—that is, enacting critical literacies to organize a radio program focused on important issues in the lives of young people—Green (2010) describes her positionality as akin to the sport of "double dutch." Like many literacy researchers, Green wears multiple hats in her research community. She is at once a participant observer, a teacher, a community organizer, and a youth advocate. Double dutch, the intricate sport of jumping between two ropes, not only involves being skillful in jumping while negotiating two ropes, but also requires an awareness of when and where to enter. Green's method, and the double-dutch metaphor, best describes my relationship to the Girl Time program. I am a Black woman, wife, mother, daughter, sister, scholar, teacher, and youth advocate, and I ache when I see the never-ending sea of black and brown faces in detention centers where Girl Time conducts playwriting and performance workshops. Therefore, my positionality is not and never can be neutral. In *The Games That Black Girls Play*, ethnomusicology scholar Kyra Gaunt (2006) asserts the intricate balancing of skills needed in double dutch, "the real art of play is learning how to get into the ropes and learning how to do a good 'dismount': exiting the ropes without interrupting their constant flow so the game can proceed seamlessly, nonstop, in the next turn" (p. 137).

I do not claim to know more than the girls we work with in the Girl Time workshops, nor the powerful team of women teaching artists who were engaged in this work long before they invited me to collaborate. I try to enter and "dismount" when and where it seems appropriate. This is the story of girls who have been "pushed out" of schools and who are trying to reenter schools, communities, a peer network, and families, as well as of the teachers who "dare to teach" them. Their stories—a balance of stories—are presented here, and while I aim to share these stories seamlessly, I know that my efforts to navigate the two ropes representing my responsibility as both a teaching artist and a scholar will inevitably collide at times. It is also important to note that I am not always the one who is jumping—I also serve as rope turner. Gaunt asserts, "the art of turning ropes . . . does lead to a sort of specialization acquired by those who are not 'double handed'" (p. 137). Green's double-dutch methodology is central to my work with Girl Time also because while double dutch is not solely played by African Americans, "it has been a cultural mainstay among black urban girls for decades" (Kelley, 1997, p. 56). In the context of Girl Time, the program serves girls from various ethnic backgrounds in the detention center facilities; however, the summer program has had only African American participants. For the purpose of this book I strive to be "double handed" and write in the rhythm of the student artists and teaching artists so as not to disrupt their cadence and flow.

Additionally I am mindful of the limitations of programs; Girl Time does not have all the answers. However, Girl Time provides an important platform to interrogate the racing, classing, and gendering of the school-to-prison pipeline. I have come to believe the frank words of scholar Ruth Nicole Brown, who argues that girls, and Black girls in particular, "need power not programs" (Brown, 2009, p. 25), which I discuss further in the fifth and final act. Thus, this work illuminates the importance of coalition building to support the personal, social, and intellectual development of girls.

Kemba's Nightmare/My Nightmare

In April 1996, *Emerge Magazine* published "Kemba's nightmare." At the time I had completed my undergraduate degree as well as my multiple and single-subject (English) teaching credentials and was enjoying the first stop on my journey as an educator in my 1st-grade classroom. Like many graduates, I temporarily moved home after college so I could save money and prepare to leave again. I can still remember seeing this issue of *Emerge* on my parents' kitchen table; it was almost as if it were strategically placed there as a reminder that as a Black woman—even with a degree—I was still not fully out of harm's way. The cover photo featured a young African American woman, Kemba Smith, in a white graduation robe and matching white graduation cap. Kemba was proudly holding a diploma and displaying a smile I had seen before; it was my smile on my graduation day and it was the smile of my friends and loved ones. Alongside the photograph was written "Kemba's Nightmare: A model child becomes Prisoner #26370-083"; underneath this headline, "Drug sentencing frenzy" and "Good kids, bad choices." I was afraid to open the magazine but like the rest of Black America I wanted to know, how did this happen? And while the second part of this question is raced, classed, and gendered, I also wanted to know, how did this happen to someone who seemed a lot like me?

The article chronicled the unlikely arrest and imprisonment of Smith, who, as a college student, became romantically involved with a young man who was dealing drugs. Ultimately, Smith—who had never had any trouble with the law—was arrested on drug charges when she was found carrying cocaine on behalf of her boyfriend. As a victim of the rigorous drug laws, Smith was initially sentenced to 23.5 years.[4] I did not see my life as being that different from Smith's and perhaps that is what frightened me the most. Coming of age in the 1980s, during the crack cocaine economy in a city that lived in the shadow of bigger cities, it was not unusual to know drug dealers. In fact, the drug dealers were my classmates and friends, and seemed like genuinely great guys. My peers and I did not have the foresight to know how this drug would eventually destroy the lives of many Black people—including people very close to me—and we did not have the language to speak out against it. I also felt that as a Black middle-class kid with active parents, I was in no position to judge my peers, who were often breadwinners in their families and caretakers of siblings their parents had left behind. This was especially true in a city where all of the Black people seemed to know one another. My parents never played the class game so I had friends with a range of lived experiences. I would be sitting next to a boy in my math class one day only to have him disappear for the next month or so. When he returned, I would learn that he was at "boys' camp" or "juvey" for dealing, and we resumed working side-by-side as if nothing happened. My friends and I would skip school in order to attend funeral services for schoolmates killed as a result of the drug trade. And while I hate to admit it (since my family may be hearing this for the first time), I was in the wrong place countless times and it is only now in my work with incarcerated and formerly incarcerated girls that I realize how incredibly naïve I was as a teen and how lucky I had been to avoid trouble.

In the context of the Girl Time program, I have a greater sense of the contrast between the girls and me. Rhodessa Jones and her co-teacher, Sean Reynolds, who work with "The Medea Project: Theater for Incarcerated Women" in the San Francisco County Jails, observe that sometimes it was plain "luck" that they, as Black women, did not find themselves suffering the same fate as the women, also mostly Black, they collaborated with in the jails:

> It's more the difference between the "privileged" and the "underserved," with us being a part of that privileged African American class who—because of timing, luck, nerve, and education of a different sort—did not wind up in jail. (Sean Reynolds, quoted in Fraden, 2001, p. 81)

While I count myself as one of the "lucky" ones, I am profoundly aware of the privilege that I live with daily. After my fellow teaching artists and I complete a workshop in the detention center, we return to our homes. After the Girl Time summer program is complete, we celebrate with our families and even take vacations or breaks from the world to clear our heads. We are on the other side of teenage decisionmaking and peer pressure, yet we must keep our memories and experiences as girls accessible to do this work with great love and with openness to what the girls have to teach us.

Traversing the Terrain

Like the writing of the girls in the Girl Time playwriting and performance program, this book is very much a series of acts and scenes played out on the stages of regional youth detention centers, moving to a multi-service center serving formerly incarcerated youth, then to a public theater, and then back to the regional youth detention centers where formerly incarcerated girls return as performers and messengers delivering the news that there is a life beyond the walls. Therefore, I view the sections of this book as Acts, as opposed to Chapters.

Act I—"Voices Can Be Heard": Theatre for Incarcerated Girls—introduces the Girl Time pedagogy. Here the pedagogical practices of the program are viewed through the lens of performance ethnography and historicizing the literacy practices of incarcerated girls. Through what the teaching artists refer to as the "verbiage" of Girl Time teaching artists and scenes from the workshops, I explore the intersection of process, product, and playmaking, and the ways in which this process supports the development of critical literacies.

In Act II—"Yes, and": Teaching Freedom in Confined Spaces—you will meet the cast from the Girl Time teaching-artist ensemble—Kaya, Anne, Zaire, Carrie Mae, Petulia, Isis, Mindy, Ginger, and Julisa—through qualitative interview data and narratives. I attempt to show how the lived experiences of this team of teachers have influenced their teaching philosophies and pedagogical practices. What is particularly compelling about this team of teachers is their diversity; they hail from various regions of the United States; they are gay, straight, single, married, mothers, and artists involved with various aspects of theatre. They range in age and have different styles. Through a close look at their stories and observed pedagogical practices, I try to provide a framework for teaching freedom even in the midst of chaos and confusion. While these teachers do their work against the backdrop of juvenile justice institutions, the constraints they endure as educators committed to providing a safety net for urban youth are not unlike those experienced by social justice educators in American public schools.

Act III—"We Try to Find Our Way Home": Formerly Incarcerated Girls Speak—introduces Nia, Sanaa, Jada, Lisa, and Janelle, who participated in the Girl Time summer program after being released from RYDCs. Formerly incarcerated girls, or the student artists, provide wisdom and insight into the social, economic, and educational issues that feed the school-to-prison pipeline. While I collected data for 3 years and interviewed many girls, I specifically focus on girls who participated in the program for multiple summers.

Act IV—The Trouble with Black Girls: Racing, Classing, and Gendering the School-to-Prison Pipeline—examines what is at stake for girls, especially girls of color in underserved communities and schools, through a review of salient research. I have organized the research in such a way that communities can use this Act as a platform to begin a dialogue for change. Act IV invites girls, their parents and guardians, teachers, school administrators and staff, and detention center administrators and staff to examine the policies and practices that contribute to the school-to-prison pipeline. This act is also an invitation to youth advocates to consider the issues that specifically impact girls.

Act V—Magic Carpets and Fairylands: Preparing for a Performance of Possibilities—begins to reimagine the world of zero-tolerance policies and increased policing of youth and rethink the ways in which various stakeholders—including the girls themselves, educators, policymakers, parents, and community members—can work together to support girls. This act also pays close attention to what happens when we actually listen to these girls, read and witness their plays, and experience their performances.

"Voices Can Be Heard"
Theatre for Incarcerated Girls

"You have 2 minutes to find out at least five differences and five similarities between you and your partner. These can't be things people can see on the outside. So you really have to talk this through." Petulia, one of the Girl Time teaching artists, explained to a group of 16 girls in an RYDC workshop. In pairs, the girls hovered over their steno note-pads sharing one dull pencil in order to begin this challenge. The minute one of these pencils rested on a table or chair unattended, a junior correctional officer (JCO) quickly confiscated it. At first Lupe and Jardin just stared at each other and then Lupe offered, "We both like fighting." Jardin agreed so Lupe wrote it down. "We both locked up," Lupe continued. "Yeah, that's true," Jardin offered. I chimed in at that point, "Remember to choose things that people cannot see or that are not obvious." Jardin asked Lupe, "Are you on probation?" Lupe nodded in affirmation and added that to the list. "Do you like football?" Jardin asked, to which Lupe responded, "Yes." "Football" was added to the list. After pairs or trios of girls shared their responses aloud, Carrie Mae, another teaching artist, offered another prewriting challenge: "Please list all of the emotions you felt at some point this week." "Oh that's easy," Lupe responded. Lupe and Jardin listed words back and forth as if they were rallying in a tennis match: frustrated, scared, outraged, depressed, lonely, discriminated against, upset, isolated, angry, ecstatic." "Ecstatic?" Jardin asked incredulously. "Yeah, when we had our butter sandwiches," Lupe recalled with a smirky grin. I had not heard of a butter sandwich, but soon learned it consisted of peanut butter, honey, and a third ingredient I cannot recall, mixed up and served on bread. Butter sandwiches were considered a real treat in the detention center and served on rare occasions. Kaya, the Girl Time program director and lead teacher, asked me to work with Lupe and Jardin during the playwriting process. Both girls were lukewarm during the warm-ups and theatre games; they did everything half-heartedly, refused to make eye contact, and leaned against the walls in a hopeless slump. However, once we got down to the business of writing a play, both girls grew excited about the possibilities.

"We can write about a girl who gets beat by her boyfriend," Lupe said while practically squirming in her chair with enthusiasm. "No, we can write about being in here," Jardin countered. Lupe, intent on her battered girlfriend storyline, replied, "No, the girl who gets beat comes in here for drug charges. And she is pregnant!" As the storylines progressed they began to get increasingly complicated. "One thing I want you to think about as you write your play," I began, "is that you have an opportunity to tell a story you have never been able to tell. You have an opportunity to create characters and introduce people who may have never met but you think should meet." There was an awkward silence and like all Girl Time teaching artists I felt continuously conflicted trying to find the balance of when and where to enter. After giving me a quizzical look, Jardin continued, "If the girl gets beaten then I want her to be able to fight back in the end." Lupe gets up and acts out a fight scene in which the girl throws punches after being punched by her boyfriend. "What is the purpose of the play? What is the message you want to convey at the end of the play?" I further probed. "I want the girl to be heard," Jardin responded. "I want the girl to be strong in the end and know that she can be heard." Lupe sat back down after her reenactment of a violent fight scene, "Well maybe she can get shot by her boyfriend and then he begins to hear voices and it's her voice." Jardin adamantly shook her head, "No, I don't think she should get killed. If we want her voice to be heard, then she needs to fight back and stay alive." Both girls looked at each other as Jardin cocked her head to the side in a pleading manner. "Okaaaaay!" Lupe surrendered, "but we better make this good. I want it to be real." Jardin snapped back, "Oh, it's going to be real and it's going to be good too!"

In a study of drama classrooms in urban high schools in Canada and New York City, Gallagher (2007) argues that drama classrooms "can be more permissive of the distinctive expressions and contributions of young people" (p. 6). Gallagher's observation can also be made of the Girl Time playwriting and performance workshops with incarcerated and formerly incarcerated girls. In the context of Girl Time, youth are invited to create a discourse of second chances; these second chances come in the form of being heard for the first time, disappearing into another character, putting people in dialogue who may or may not have ever spoken before, and charting a new path through the creation of an alternative life ending or beginning. Playwriting and theatre pedagogy, then, "is a space of many chances, many possible directions, many aborted plans, many reconsidered choices" (Gallagher, p. 23). The purpose of this act is to describe the Girl Time process beginning with RYDC workshops leading to the summer program for girls who have been released. This act will also explore theories of play in order to understand its critical role in the lives of incarcerated and formerly incarcerated girls. Lupe and Jardin, in the opening vignette, struggled with the opportunity to write a play that ended with a possible beginning. Both girls were locked into a narrow view of realness being defined as abuse, violence, and even death. Playwriting, according to Girl Time teaching artists, was potentially a tool for girls to write themselves out of the cycle of abuse. Jardin's yearning for her protagonist, who they named Neveah, to live and be heard was embedded in her own desire to make decisions that could transform her life in positive ways. And while Lupe and Jardin's new vision for the play, entitled "Voices Can Be Heard," was not Lupe's original definition of "real," it became a shared vision of what was possible. This "performance of possibilities," according to Madison (2005), includes "creation and change . . . merging text with the world . . . and critically traversing the margin and the center (p. 172)." In the opening scene of "Voices Can Be Heard," Neveah's mother visits the protagonist in a youth detention center where Neveah is incarcerated. Neveah's mother is encouraging her daughter to "get her life together," especially since she has a baby at home. Part of getting her life together, according to Neveah's mother, means leaving Luis, her abusive boyfriend, behind. When Neveah gets out of the detention center she moves in with Luis, against her mother's wishes, and quickly learns she has made a mistake. After a physical altercation resulting in Luis knocking Neveah to the ground, she decides she must get her baby and leave. Jardin and Lupe chose to have the narrator close the story; however, as the narrator begins to tell about Neveah's new life, the narrator's voice is replaced by

Neveah's voice (this is physically represented on stage by Neveah and the narrator overlapping lines while Neveah enters stage right and the narrator exiting stage left). The audience soon realizes that Neveah is speaking to a group of girls in a youth detention center facility much like where Lupe and Jardin write their play. Neveah appeals to the group of girls to have the courage to walk away from physically and emotionally abusive relationships:

> I am happy to be out of domestic violence and drug abuse. And happy my daughter will not grow up in that situation. I promised myself I'd never come back to [Main RYDC], but here I am telling you young girls how your voices can be heard.

Prewriting, ensemble building, physical warm-ups, and theatre games are essential to the Girl Time workshops whether they occur in a Regional Youth Detention Center (RYDC), community center, school, the multi-service center, or in the theatre itself. The role of play cannot be underestimated in young lives. In a testing climate in which young people are experiencing "circuits of dispossession" and being tested—and consequently punished for not passing these tests (Fine & Ruglis, 2009), the word *play* might elicit a collective sigh recalling days past. Play has been theorized by many; however, Vygotsky's notion of play as "the first emancipation from situational constraints" is salient to understanding the pedagogy of playwriting and performance in incarcerated and formerly incarcerated girls' lives (Vygotsky, 1978, p. 99). According to Vygotsky, play "teaches [a child] to desire by relating her desires to a fictitious 'I,' to her role in the game and its rules" (p. 100).

In Girl Time workshops, student artists play. Student artists and teaching artists engage in physical warm-ups, theatre games, and eventually playwriting and performing through which they get to create characters and dialogue, become different characters, and articulate a new desire of who they want to be or of the lives they wish to have. Through "performing writing and literacy," these girls are in fact rehearsing new desires (Fishman, Lunsford, McGregor, & Otuteye, 2005). The role of rehearsal is to cultivate a performance of possibilities. Fraden (2001) reminds us of the origins of the word *rehearse*, "to harrow—the act of using a tool that works like a rake, leveling and breaking up plowed ground, covering seeds, rooting up weeds" (p. 69). In The Medea Project: Theater for Incarcerated Women, co-founder and performance artist Rhodessa Jones understands role playing and the intersection of education, therapy, and art as "creative survival" (p. 76). Arguing that women do not simply go to jail because of crime, Jones posits that people go to jail due to "poverty, sickness, all that stems from pain and loss and lack of self esteem . . . and in the course of time, nobody—their captors, the gatekeepers, the keyholders—gets [incarcerated people] to tell their story" (p. 77). However, people released from detention centers, jails, and prisons are expected to return and integrate without having time and space to rehearse for the real.

Like Jones' work with incarcerated women in San Francisco County jails, Boal's Theatre of the Oppressed (TOP) views theatre as "the representation of the real" (Boal, 2006, p. 109). Boal's theatre work in prisons further supports the notion that Lupe, Jardin, and other girls' playwriting and performances have to be a process that prepares them for life beyond the youth detention center. "In prison," according to Boal, "one is preparing to return to social life, to society. This return to the world outside needs to be rehearsed inside the walls" (p. 110). For Lupe and Jardin to choose to make their young female protagonist leave an abusive partner and become a resource to other incarcerated girls was a bold step toward rehearsing and redefining the real. Like Boal, Girl Time teaching artists ask how the incarcerated will shed the scarlet letter branded on them and engraved in their records as they prepare for life beyond a particular choice made in a particular context or a situation that felt as if they had no choices at all. This is an even more compelling question for incarcerated children. Educators who are teaching dignity and humanity while teaching their content area have much in common with these Freirian teachers:

> Our work in the prison must look forward to his/her possible life, after prison. We have to use theatre to deal with his/her present oppressions, in prison, and to conjecture his/her future oppressions, in freedom. (Boal, 2006, p. 115)[1]

Incarcerated girls in the Girl Time workshops have learned that a hasty decision or indecision can often have severe consequences including being jailed, isolation from family and friends, a disruption in schooling, and overall uncertainty. All of this is experienced during a developmental period in which youth are trying to make meaning of their lives and formulate their identities. However, there is an opportunity in the pedagogy of playwriting and performance to transform experiences into something tangible and worthy of being shared:

What we experience is most often whatever needed to be expressed . . .
experience made into expression brings forth reader, observer, listener,
village, community, and audience . . . experience becomes the very seed
of performance. (Madison, 2005, pp. 151–152)

The writing process in a pedagogy that promotes a performance of
possibilities begins long before the girls gather around their shared note-
pads and pencils. As soon as girls are brought on the unit or into the space
where the workshop is held, they are introduced to a series of physical
warm-ups and theatre games to begin the process of building ensemble.
Girl Time teaching artists immediately introduce themselves to the girls
writing out name tags for everyone. Every gesture is purposeful; teachers
make the first move by walking up to each girl to introduce themselves
and are deliberately mindful not to huddle in an all-teacher circle. Teaching artists always make sure that they have a girl on either side of them
during the warm-up activities. Kaya, the Girl Time program director who
you will meet in Act II, offers the welcome:

We are Girl Time and we are so happy and honored to be with
you today. We are a group of women in the theatre arts who care
deeply about women and girls. We support women and girls'
voices and stories.

Voice, or the notion of voice, is often overused if not misunderstood.
Literacy research has helped shift the idea of educators giving voice to
youth (and marginalized youth in particular) to a more nuanced understanding that youth come to formal and informal spaces of learning with
powerful voices and ideas. Rather than needing "voice," most youth need
a space, an opportunity, and an engaged audience so they can share their
voices. Performance ethnography defines voice as an "embodied, historical self that constructs and is constructed by a matrix of social and political processes" (Madison, 2005, p. 173). Therefore, voice is not neutral;
it is a complex intersection of how one views him- or herself as well as
how one is viewed by external forces. "Voice" is consistently referenced
in the Girl Time verbiage (and further discussed by teaching artists in
the next act). Because Girl Time is housed in a woman-focused theatre
company committed to producing the work of women playwrights and/
or plays with compelling female characters, the teaching artist verbiage
is more than lip service. Our Place Theatre Company, which houses Girl
Time, has as its mission to produce the work of women playwrights and/

or plays that have compelling roles for women. Our Place also hosts an annual "Women in the Arts" luncheon as well as a playwriting festival for women playwrights. Through physical warm-ups, theatre games, and exercises, girls' and women's voices, sounds, and movements create a space for taking chances, displaying vulnerability, and fostering a connection between the fluid roles of "teacher" and "student." Voice is cultivated through activities and nurtured in the circle of girls and women.

Warming Up with Girl Time

Stepping into the middle of the circle, Kaya or another teacher begins the warm-up with the question, "Who can name some athletic balls?" Girls begin to shout out names of balls such as tennis balls, basketballs, volleyballs, footballs, Ping Pong balls, and kickballs:

> Okay, now I want you to think of something that upset you this week or frustrated you. . . . On the count of three, using a sound and a movement, you are going to shape that problem into one of the balls we listed. So if it's a big problem you may have to create a beach ball or if it's a smaller problem you may only need to shape it in the size of a tennis ball. Show us that ball.
>
> Since we have a lot of fun and hard work ahead of us today we need to get that negative ball of energy out of this circle so we can start fresh with each other. We are going to need to work together as a team—as an ensemble. On the count of three, using a sound and movement, we are going to throw that negative thing out of this circle! Ready? 1— 2— 3!

Everyone dramatizes throwing their ball out of the circle. Some get creative and wind up their arms while others opt to kick the ball away.

> Whew! Now let's focus on something good or something positive that happened or will happen and let's rub our hands together as we think about that positive energy. We are going to pass that positive energy around in the form of a clap. I'm going to turn to my neighbor on the right, make eye contact, and we will clap together and she will pass it around.

As the clap makes itself around the circle there are smiles, laughter, or even very serious looks. Some girls get visibly annoyed if they sense one of their peers is not moving fast enough or if they perceive a disruption in the rhythm. Teaching artists recognize this frustration and remind the circle, "Listen for the rhythm. It's not about speed. It's about us establishing a rhythm together." Eye contact is one the most important aspects of this activity and is the way teachers encourage student artists to say, "Here I am. Look at me." This is the making of an ensemble and every warm-up, game, and activity builds from this.

Pass the clap is always followed by the name game. Just as the eye contact in many ways says, "I am here and I am present," saying and showing one's name during the name game invites girls to further vocalize their presence in the circle and the world. If voice is "the presentation of a historical self" and, thus, "a full presence that is in and of a particular world" (Madison, 2005, p. 173), the name game in many ways is the crowning jewel for the prewriting process. During the name game, girls are invited to show their names using their body, a movement, and the space around them. Teaching artists have their own creative ways of introducing the experience. Zaire, who you will learn more about in Act II, typically leads the name game:

> Your name is something that no one can ever take away from you. Sometimes we don't like our names but we have to claim them and say them in a way that people know how we feel about ourselves. I know you can do it. Show us what you got. (Field notes, summer 2009)

In her work with urban youth, Christensen (2000) asserts that naming is, perhaps, the most important place for teachers to begin a relationship with students and for students to cultivate relationships with their peers. Naming has such profound significance in indigenous communities and for people of color because of the ways names and titles have been imposed on poor people of color in urban America. Some girls have no trouble showing their name with a loud, clear voice punctuated by a memorable movement, but others struggle. The circle is the safety net, and if a girl struggles with this exercise we go back to her. Beginning with girls' voices is central to Girl Time pedagogy. It would be irresponsible not to historicize these young lives (Gutiérrez, 2008). These girls are primarily African American, growing up in an urban southeastern city, attending decaying public schools, yet they are descendants of a long line of Black women who make a way out of no way through speaking, performing, and using their voices and bodies as tools and weapons (Winn, 2010b).

"We All Have a Past": Staged Readings

After the warm-ups, teaching artists do a staged reading of two plays, "Ghosts of the Past" and "Beauty and the Thug," written by incarcerated girls in the Girl Time RYDC workshops. "Ghosts" tells the story of a young woman haunted by her past as she prepares to marry the man of her dreams. Waiting for a phone call from her wedding florist, Monica receives a call from Dre who was one of her past partners in crime. Dre threatens to tell Monica's fiancé, Robert, that she comes with a past including serving prison time for murder. If this story seems unlikely I found it uncanny when I came across Piper Kerman's (2010) compelling memoir *Orange Is the New Black: My Year in Women's Prison*. Kerman served a 1-year sentence for a crime she committed right out of college some 10 years earlier. Like Monica, Kerman had to explain this predicament to her significant other and their families. Monica decides to tell her fiancé about her past before Dre does, and, as one can imagine, he first thinks she is joking before becoming outraged. At the end of "Ghosts," Monica is packing her things when her fiancé returns to give her and their relationship a second chance (see Appendix A).

"Beauty and the Thug" is an urban fairytale set in the land of "Koolash." Told by a narrator (physically represented on stage by an actor sitting in a chair reading from a large book) this play depicts a princess who is to marry a prince whom she does not love. The princess becomes enamored by an everyday "thug" who "happened upon her." Reading all of the thug's actions incorrectly—partially because she takes his metaphorical word play a bit too literally—the princess decides to end her engagement to the prince and pursue a life with the thug. Peabo, the thug, tells the princess, "Hold up, Shawty! Where is all this coming from?" In other words, Peabo has no idea how and why the princess thinks they have a future together. Analese, the princess, is left with a broken heart and the narrator leaves the audience with a moral to the story, "You can bring a thug into a fairytale but he will still be a thug" (see Appendix B).

Every staged reading is followed by a talk-back with the girls, which Kaya typically begins by asking girls what they liked about the plays. Isis, one of the teaching artists you will also meet in Act II, played Monica and another teaching artist, Mindy, also participated in the talk-back:

> *Student artist*: I like Robert because he is the romantic type and I like the "G"[2] too because he was real.

Student artist: You see that every day. That's how dudes approach
    females and they fall for it. It's complicated.
Student artist: I like the princess—she was sad and the thug was
    mean and grouchy like my mom and grandma.
Student artist: I like Isis' scene (Isis played Monica)—it would
    take a lot to tell your husband you murdered somebody.
Student artist: [I like] Isis' character. We all have a past.
Student artist: The fact that [Monica] stood up to the dude on the
    phone and said "No," was good.

One of the student artists moved one of the heavy chairs (we learned
were filled with sand so none of the children could pick it up and use it as
a weapon) across the room so Isis could have a seat. We all thanked her.

Student artist: I liked the princess because she was willing to give
    up her crown for love. I like Robert for not judging.
Student artist: I like the princess because she was talking to the
    flowers. That reminds me of me.
Everyone laughed.
Student artist: Well I saw the princess as showing how girls throw
    something good away to people who don't deserve it.
Kaya: It forces me to think about what I am willing to give up.
    These plays were written at Main RYDC by girls on the unit.

At this point the girls looked at each other with disbelief and some
leaned forward in their chairs. Many girls wanted to continue talking
about the plays.

Student artist: "Beauty and the Thug" reminds me of the movie
    Why Did I Get Married? and the *80/20 Rule*. It's like you chase
    20% when you already had 80% and you end up with either
    20 or nothing.
Kaya: What percent are you keeping for you?
Isis: No one can give you 100%. You have to keep some for
    yourself.
Student artist: I don't understand "Ghosts of the past." How did
    that guy find her? Who was he?
Mindy: He was like her pimp. She tricked for him, made money
    for him and he was looking for her to come back and do the
    same things she was doing.

A different student artist turned to the one who asked the question and followed up with, "Do you understand now?"

> *Kaya*: I appreciate you asking questions. That's really important that we've created a safe space in here to ask questions. (Field notes, January 29, 2008).

When Kaya reveals to the girls that both plays were written by incarcerated girls in RYDCs it is as if all of the girls' faces light up. RYDCs are, in theory, transitional facilities where youth are detained as they await court dates, decisions about their placements (serving more time at another facility, foster care, group homes, halfway houses, and sometimes home). Tensions and emotions are high as there is so much uncertainty. Since boys still outnumber girls in youth arrests and detainment, girls are like an island surrounded by a sea of boys. The thought of writing a play sometimes inspires a good laugh initially; however, even when we begin with reluctant participants, it is telling that by the end of day one of the workshop everyone has written a play.

Building Sandcastles: The Road to Writing

In the opening scene in this act you meet Lupe and Jardin as well as teaching artists, Petulia and Carrie Mae. You also get a glimpse of the work that takes place the first day of the RYDC workshop. Once students and teachers have engaged in games, activities, the staged reading, and a talkback, student artists—as I have come to refer to the girls who participate in the Girl Time workshops—are counted and partnered with one to two other people. One teaching artist works with a pair or trio; however, it is important to note that teaching artists serve as more of a facilitator. They are available for questions, encouragement, and even to transcribe the plays as the girls dictate. Some student artists are ready to write after seeing "Ghosts" and "Beauty" while others are just warming up to the idea. Before Lupe and Jardin began writing their play, they explored their similarities and differences as well as a range of emotions they experienced. These student artists also had to imagine being stranded on an island together with only an empty coffee can and its lid in their possession. Some of the more popular uses student artists come up with include using the can to catch fish, store food, and play drums (you have to have music everywhere!). However, there have been some other ideas for usage as well, like building sandcastles and catching butterflies. It is in these moments that girls and women are temporarily transported above the buzz of secured doors, these same doors slamming shut at least a thousand times in the short period we are there, and the static from the JCO's radios. We can never forget where these initial workshops take place—we are in a jail for children—and on many occasions we are reminded of that by emergency counts, girls coming and going in order to attend court dates, and sometimes very triumphant moments when girls return from court to announce they are "going home." We are always humbled by girls who go to court, return with news that they have to serve more time in a facility miles away from their families, and yet still want to finish their plays and performances.

As the activities build toward writing a play, student artists brainstorm and explore different relationships. In pairs or in trios, they create a list of relationships including inanimate objects, like a sock and a shoe, or human relationships, like mother and daughter, teacher and student, or best friends. More recently one of the teaching artists thought there was still one more step missing before girls began writing their plays and suggested we offer an exercise to put a relationship example "on its feet." As an ensemble we choose one of the relationship pairs, take volunteers to play the roles and feed lines in order to create an impromptu scene from a play. Plays are written on the first day in about 2 hours, relationship seeds are planted, and we complete read-throughs of each play. Kaya makes an announcement that girls will be cast in plays other than the ones they wrote. This always invokes a bit of disappointment for girls who have become attached to the characters they have created:

> You are playwrights. It is a gift to a playwright to be able to sit
> back and really see and hear your play. I know you are invested
> in your characters, but I promise you that you will be just as in-
> vested in them when someone performs them (Field notes,
> August 30, 2006).

Throughout the first day of the workshop Kaya observes, sits in with different groups and notes each girl's strengths, who may want larger roles, and who may be a struggling reader and need roles with less dialogue. Some girls inform us if they prefer minimal roles and Kaya always asks who would be comfortable playing male characters. And like teachers everywhere, Girl Time teaching artists have homework that night. Teaching artists type plays that night and part of the work is keeping the girls' language intact. There is no censoring, with the exception of following the rules of the RYDCs, which prohibit the n-word and profanity. On the second day of the workshop, girls receive their roles and teaching artists are assigned plays to direct. In theatre, language must be authentic—there is room for African American vernacular English, Spanish, Creole, and southern swagger. Plays include *y'all*, *scrait* for *straight* (as in, "I'm straight" or "I'm good"), and even concepts like "ride or die," which I discuss extensively in Act III. Keeping language intact is a way to build trust by acknowledging there are other "Englishes" in the world (Poppa Joe in Fisher, 2007). In performance ethnography, language is viewed as performative, "Language does more than describe; it also does something that makes material, physical, and situational difference" (Madison, 2005, p. 161). Both "Ghosts" and "Beauty" use language with specific intentions. The ending of "Ghosts" is indicative of many of the play endings written by incarcerated girls; typically things work out for the best because in the confines of a detention center children must believe they will be free, forgiven, and even provided with opportunities to make informed decisions. In the talk-back, student artists always express their fondness for the character Robert in "Ghosts" because he makes the ultimate decision, which is to forgive Monica and give her a chance. Madison further argues, "The words, 'You are forgiven' all do something in the world. They create a particular reality. Language can bestow forgiveness, a blessing, freedom, citizenship, marriage, or a promise. Language performs a reality" (p. 161).

Speaking Up and Talking Back: Actors and "Spectactors"

When girls receive their scripts on the second day—both the scripts for plays in which they have been cast as well as plays they coauthored, these pieces of paper are coveted. On the second day plays are blocked—a process that I continue to stumble through awkwardly—in which the cast practices how the dialogue is physically represented on stage. Teaching artists, now serving as directors, make decisions about where actors will stand, when and where they will enter and move, and where props (minimal—typically, a couple of plastic chairs) are placed. The second day can also be a highly emotional day; during the first day, Kaya gets the names of parents and guardians whom the girls want us to contact and invite to the performance that closes the second day. Some girls are devastated if no one from their family can attend, and this is where we see ensemble at work. Girls encourage each other—"Girl, you doin' this for you! Not for them!" One couple started attending all the workshops at one of the RYDCs to be surrogate audience members for girls whose families could not attend. Teaching artists invite friends, families, and significant others to ensure there will be an audience.

Every performance ends with a "talk-back." During this talk-back, guardians, families, and detention center staff get to engage with the student artists about their work. Zaire began this particular talk-back at Main RYDC by asking the girls if there were any challenges during the process. Some of the girls shared that it was hard to "keep going when you mess up." One student artist shared, "having confidence in yourself."

Zaire: Was there anything you learned?
Student artist: How to act it out.
Student artist: You learn how to express yourself.
Student artist: I learned how to write a play!
The teaching artists cheered.
Student artist: It felt better to watch someone else do my play because I would have been too embarrassed to do it myself.
Zaire: That is very important.
Kaya: I think you are the first person to share that.
Zaire: This is why we ask you to perform in another play because it is an honor as a playwright to watch your play performed by others.
Student artist: I learned that everybody got talent in here.
Everyone cheered.
Zaire: This question is for the audience, the families, and the girls too. Were there any topics that made you pause? I know there were some for me.
A mother: I liked the "Ride or Die." It makes you think what these boys think and the girl did not let herself get in trouble for the guy.
Zaire: This was one of the first plays where the girl was not the sacrificial lamb.
Audience member: I liked "Hair Drama." It was creative and mature.
Zaire: It made you think out of the box.
Student artist: I liked "Baby's Momma Drama" because the woman still stayed with her husband even though he wasn't right.
Maisha (responding to the student artist): You know something Titi, I noticed that you shared something similar yesterday about "Ghosts of the Past" and that helps me see something beautiful in you and your power to forgive.

Zaire: We have to learn how to accept compliments because we always hear what people don't like about us but never what people like. You think your circumstances control you but remember they cannot house your creativity. They cannot lock down your souls and spirit. You can still write. You can write poetry.

A mother: Just because you made bad choices doesn't mean you cannot change.

Zaire: It's not even about bad choices because all of us have made bad choices at some time. You can look in the mirror and ask yourself, "Did I make a *positive* choice today?" We hope to see you on the outside. Don't let this be the last time we see you doing something good. (Field notes, February 20, 2007)

While the second day of the Girl Time RYDC workshops may seem like the end, it is really the beginning for some girls who participate in the summer program upon their release. As an ethnographer and teaching artist, the ability to experience the pedagogy of Girl Time in RYDCs while girls are incarcerated and during the summer after girls have been released is a rich opportunity to consider how teaching freedom is possible and necessary in jails and beyond.

The Journey Toward "Home"

The strength of multi-sited ethnographic fieldwork is that I followed girls through their process. This is important because I did not interview girls in detention centers, I conducted interviews with girls in a multi-service center serving formerly incarcerated youth after they were released (I discuss this more in Act III). Multi-sited ethnographic fieldwork also allowed me to follow the life of a play—from ensemble building and brainstorming, to the actual writing and "putting it on its feet" for an RYDC performance as well as the public performance during the summer program. Summer is sweltering in the southeast and, in spite of the heat, formerly incarcerated girls and teaching artists convene on a Sunday afternoon to launch the summer program. For 7 days that lead to a Saturday public performance, plus a tour day when the show goes on the road to different detention centers, student artists continue physical warm-ups, games, and activities they encountered in the RYDC workshops, in addition to very specific theatre techniques and practices for actors. Layli, a real stage manager from the theatre that provides the space for the public performance (for free!), introduces girls to theatre etiquette as she collects valuables, goes over the daily agenda, and makes sure everybody adheres to the time. Girls are treated as professionals; they are expected to be on time and present daily. While their pay is a humble stipend of $100, it is greatly appreciated by the girls and their guardians especially when most of the youth summer programs in the city can cost up to $2000 to participate. Every summer the show is "sold out," and the theatre reaches its capacity of 202 (and perhaps a few more). During the last two summers, Girl Time invited people to watch the dress rehearsal to accommodate everyone who wished to attend. While the first 5 days of the summer program are held at a multi-service center, the last 2 take place in the theatre Layli calls "home." She welcomes Girl Time:

> Welcome to my home. This is a very special place. This is my home. I've worked here for 9 years and I've spent ninety five percent of my time in this city in this building. I'm sharing my home with you, so please respect it . . . throw away your trash and basically use the same judgment you would make when visiting someone's home. Breathe in and take in the love. Breathe out and share the love with someone else . . . (Field notes, June 20, 2008)

In addition to following the work of formerly incarcerated girls, their writing, and performances, this multi-sited ethnography also allowed me to follow the work of the teaching ensemble. In the next act, I introduce the teaching philosophy of Girl Time, as well as the diverse stories, teaching philosophies, and pedagogical practices of the Girl Time teaching artists.

"Yes, and"

Teaching Freedom in Confined Spaces

One swampy hot day in late August 2006, I made my way to a regional youth detention center in an urban southeastern city. As I approached the facility I noticed how the lush green pines that were a signature of the region did not manage to camouflage the spiraling barbed wire topping an endless chain link fence. This was the time of year in my California childhood that I would be preparing for the first day of school, looking forward to wearing a new, perfectly coordinated outfit, and excited about seeing my friends. On this day, however, I was preparing to enter a jail for children. These children were not preparing for their first day of school. They were getting ready for other transitions, such as court dates, transfers to long-term detention facilities, group homes or foster care, and sometimes preparing to return to their homes and communities. On this summer day I joined a community of teachers who were committed to improving the lives of girls and women through the theatre arts. And this was my first workshop.

Kaya, the Girl Time program director and lead teacher, welcomed me to my first RYDC workshop with her bright smile and introduced me to the other teaching artists who were working that day. We were informed that I had to complete my orientation prior to participating in the workshop. During my "orientation," Ms. Redd, the volunteer services coordinator, took me down each hallway of the facility. She explained that the facility held 200 detainees but could hold 400 if they "doubled up" or put two in each room. Young people who committed any of the "seven deadly sins" (yes, this is the official language), including murder, attempted murder, armed robbery, rape, child molestation, and other violent crimes had to have their own room. I asked her how many young people were detained at that time and she said approximately 230. Ms. Redd also explained that they only had space for about 50 girl detainees. As we walked through the halls I noticed banners and posters with daily affirmations somehow fastened to the painted cinder block walls. We peeked in the "school" window; all detainees attended school year-round and according to Ms. Redd all the teachers had to be "certified." Ms. Redd pointed out male and female detainees with goldenrod t-shirts in a sea of children wearing navy blue. "Gold shirts" represented good behavior and privileges included access to common areas with carpet and chairs with cushions. It was difficult to ignore the fact that most, if not all, of the faces were brown. These faces stared at me as I stared back at them. Smiling uncomfortably, I did not know if I was supposed to be friendly or not. While I hated to admit it, some of the classrooms I saw looked like some classrooms I have seen in public schools and in some cases a bit better. There was a small library, a full-time librarian, and lots of colorful posters adorning the rooms. One male detainee walked toward the window as he saw us and tried to get Ms. Redd's attention, to which she responded, "The answer is 'No!' and you know why after how you were acting yesterday. No! You are not supposed to be walking around during class." Ms. Redd explained to me, "They are in here because they did something wrong but they always try to blame everyone else. I am a 'no' person all the way because you have to be consistent. They are here because no one was consistent with them . . . I used to stay long hours and do extra programs for them, but they did not appreciate it and I could be spending that time with my son."

As we continued our tour, a line of detainees in navy blue jumpsuits walked by us; girls were in the front of the line and boys were in the back. All of the children had their arms behind their backs with their wrists perfectly stacked and aligned as if they were wearing handcuffs in spite of the fact they were not. Perhaps the handcuffs in their minds were more effective than the real thing. One boy waited at the door as we approached, hoping to hold it open for us until Ms. Redd instructed him to shut the door. Girls were not only outnumbered but practically surrounded in this largely male world. By the time I completed the orientation I was disoriented. Ms. Redd's world of "No" was a stark contrast to Girl Time's "Yes, and . . . " teaching philosophy. Kaya had just shared the foremost pedagogical practice of the program: "Remember today we have to be very positive . . . We have to affirm everything positive [the girls] do today. Remember to say, 'Yes, and,' because we are trying to validate their ideas and help them extend their ideas as well."

Girl Time is the culmination of coalition building and a chorus of girls' and women's voices and actions as described in the first act. Among the teaching-artist team is the collective wisdom of actors (stage, film, television, and commercial), costume designers, directors, teachers of youth, adults, elders, organizers of creativity and imagination workshops, and advocates for girls and women. Teaching artists—all women—touch everything from women's reproductive rights, HIV education, and sex and sexuality education to youth radio and youth advocacy. Ethnically the team is diverse by southeastern standards; teaching artists identify themselves as either African American or White and, more recently, Latina. When the teaching team walks into a youth detention center workshop housing a mostly Black population of boys, girls, and an all Black staff, they are regarded with great suspicion. Girls cock their heads to the side while others seem amused. At times girls are shy and surprised by how quickly the teachers assemble around them asking their names, introducing themselves, and filling out name tags for them. Once the team begins to engage the girls with the physical warm-ups and games, the incredulous looks slowly disappear. When the teaching team works with the girls, they are so focused that it is as if nothing and no one matters, even as the constant static reverberates from junior correctional officers' (JCOs') radios. After a while the girls seem oblivious to the snickers from passing boys, which are quickly replaced by yearning voices asking, "Why don't you ever come work with the boys?" Kaya, Girl Time's program director, and I still marvel over a conversation we had with an RYDC administrator. This particular facility contracted out to a private firm specializing in jails for children.[1] Once this administrator learned we were working with girls he expressed his enthusiasm, "We just don't know what to do with the girls . . . boys are easy but the girls are so different and complicated." Seemingly unaware he was talking to a group of women, the administrator continued, "And the girls have too many problems!"

While the boys' sense of longing to be included in the program is understandable, the program maintains that incarcerated boys have a range of activities to choose from while the girls' options are along the lines of "getting their hair done." Many of the girls in the detention centers express their dislike for "other females." One Girl Time teaching artist who you meet in this act, Mindy, observed, "The girls use the word 'female' as if it were profanity and the worst thing you could be." Indeed, "I don't like that female" and "I hate being around all these females" are declarations that affirm why the teaching artists do this work. Part of the ensemble work in Girl Time workshops is about rebuilding trust between girls and women, among mothers and daughters, grandmothers and granddaughters, partners, and friends.

The purpose of this act is to introduce the core team of Girl Time teaching artists. Through the narratives of Kaya, Anne, Zaire, Carrie Mae, Petulia, Isis, Mindy, Ginger, and Julisa, as well as their lived experiences, you will learn how they developed and continuously revisited their teaching philosophy (or philosophies) in the context of their work with incarcerated and formerly incarcerated girls. These Freirian teaching artists are, of course, unique, and each of their pedagogical portraits offers both a mirror and a window for educators who work in oppressive and marginalized spaces. While remaining committed to teaching freedom, Girl Time teaching artists' lives demonstrate the range of experiences, dispositions, and strategies educators brought to this work. What these educators share is the desire and yearning for girls and women to have multiple forums to tell, write, perform, and revise their stories and have multiple forums and venues to do so. They also share the desire to have audiences who will engage, question, and think about the ways they can contribute to improving the lives of girls and women. While their voices and stories are primarily featured in this chapter, they will be echoed throughout the rest of the book.

I spent an average of 1.5 hours for each of the nine teaching artists interviewed and profiled in this chapter. All interviews were conducted in my home, videotaped, digitized using iMovie and iDVD, and transcribed. During the digitizing process I created chapters to correspond to the themes I found in my analysis of interview data. Teachers were given their pedagogical portraits and able to review quotes. Interviews with Kaya, the Girl Time program director, and Anne, the Our Place artistic director and Girl Time co-founder, lasted 2 hours because they were my sources for the program history.

Daring to Teach

In his "Letters to those who dare to teach," Freire (1998) challenges educators to grapple with the "dynamic relationship between what we inherit and what we acquire" (p. 124). Girl Time's ensemble of teaching artists collectively have traveled the world and represent the many family structures, value systems, and democratic engagement that make up the fabric of America. As an ensemble of women teaching artists, they have acquired the desire to listen to incarcerated and formerly incarcerated girls. They have also purposefully transformed the way they see and understand incarcerated and formerly incarcerated girls in order to hear the multiple stories of girls in the program. Playwriting, ensemble building, and performing are mediating tools used to excavate the stubborn walls of generalizations and stereotypes. Acquiring such skills is a decision an educator must make, for it is not always inherited. Through the activity of playwriting, Girl Time teaching artists witness the decisions girls must make daily that could mean the difference between detention and freedom, dependence and independence, and sometimes living and dying. Critical literacies, in the context of incarcerated and formerly incarcerated girls' lives is "understanding social context, moving with others and not alone" (Fraden, 2001, p. 70) and central to Girl Time pedagogy. In this work, educators "will transform the oppressed and apathetic into people who believe they can think and thus act for themselves and others" (Fraden, 2001, p. 70).

Girl Time's teaching philosophy, the "Yes, *and* . . . " philosophy, as I have come to call it, is in stark contrast to the sounds of gates and doors slamming, emergency counts, lockdowns, body searches, and the incessant world of "No, you can't," "No, you are not," and "No, you never will be." "Yes, *and*" is literally and figuratively the core of Girl Time. First there is the inquiry-based use of the phrase as in, "Yes, you have a great idea *and* now I want you to push, to challenge yourself, *and* I ask you to think outside your box. What else? There is more." Next, there is the "Yes, *and* . . . " that builds confidence, as in "Yes, your opinion is valued here *and* I want you to be open to other opinions as well" and "Yes, *and* you are right even in this place of wrong." Additionally, there is the "Yes, *and*" that honors endurance and resilience as in "Yes, *and* keep going. I got you. You won't fall because I have your back so step out and commit." Finally, "Yes, *and*" is a reminder to teachers that we serve youth who are very familiar with "NO!" Keeping "Yes, *and*" at the center of their teaching is how teachers continue to grow, inspire, question, model, support, and demonstrate their love of youth and youth justice.

"A House Where You Are Called": Kaya

"I never really wanted to teach or thought I was going to teach, but really felt a calling as it kept coming to me," explained Kaya, Girl Time's program director and lead teacher. "And I come from a family—my father was in the ministry and so was my mother—I lived in a house where you were led. It wasn't about income, it was about helping other people. I think I watched [my parents] put their words into action." A native of the urban southeast and youngest of six siblings, Kaya headed West not too long after graduating with a double major in marketing and theatre. As Kaya pursued her acting career in southern California, she found herself adding teaching jobs to her schedule. Teaching imagination workshops with neuropsychology patients eventually expanded into similar work in the Los Angeles City Schools.

> And then at the same time I was working with a company called Unusual Suspects. For 8 years, in east LA, we went into juvenile facilities and worked with boys who were incarcerated for murder. We worked with them for 3 months at a time, and they would write a full-length play and then we would produce the play in the chapel there on site.

Kaya was an "unusual suspect" to the youth as well. Kaya's small frame contained an indomitable spirit and passion for fairness and justice. When she locked her piercing blue eyes on someone, it was as if no one or nothing else existed or mattered. I was amazed at how she could stay in the room, in the moment, with an intense focus on the young people before her. Kaya believed in accountability and insisted on excellence from all of her students. While the youth Kaya worked with were typically amused that this White woman with blonde ringlets dared to step into their world, Kaya's desire for them to do and be their best would trump their initial impressions. Girls in the Girl Time program always liked Kaya because she was "fair" and "the same with everybody." It was during her work with Unusual Suspects that Kaya witnessed the injustices of the California juvenile justice system; boys—all Black and Latino—who had yet to be convicted got "stuck" in the facilities waiting for court dates. "These boys should not have been in this temporary facility," Kaya explained with urgency in her voice, "Some of them were in this 'holding pen' for 3 or 4 years." During a conversation with her father, Kaya marveled over how much time she was teaching in addition to her film and television work. "Teaching is what made me tick—what excited me. And there was huge passion there." When Kaya moved back to her birthplace she continued acting as she started a family. Ironically, one of the many roles Kaya landed was a role in the film *Hope and Redemption: The Lena Baker Story* about the first woman—African American—to be executed by the electric chair in the state of Georgia.

Eventually Kaya met Anne, the artistic director of Our Place Theatre Company, which housed Girl Time, who directed her in a play. Anne's theatre company, Our Place Theatre Company, launched Girl Time and Anne was looking for a few good women. "Anne and I just really clicked. We speak the same language." Kaya appreciated the balance of writing and performing in Girl Time. From her work in southern California detention centers, she experienced tensions between the playwrights and actors who served as teaching artists:

> I'm not a writer. And that's what I used to say because I'd be in
> there with all these professional writers, [and] it was a constant
> battle because these writers would want to just tweak the work
> and tweak the work. And I said, "It's got to be balanced. You
> have to allow time for them to act it and work on it as actors." I
> was kind of against the intense writing process . . . yes, they've
> written a great, grand piece but they've had so little time to get it
> in their mouths and their bodies.

Preserving the integrity of students writing their pieces and keeping their voices intact, in addition to breathing life into the writing through performance, was the balance Kaya was seeking. When she and Anne met and discussed the pedagogy of Girl Time, they agreed that they wanted to push "playwriting as a vehicle" to "find voice"; however, voice included the physical performance as much as the words that made up the script:

> I think especially girls of the ages we are working with have
> been stampeded, stampeded by boys . . . Anyway, I think by
> finding their voice, and playwriting as a vehicle for that, is get-
> ting back in touch with their impulses of who they are . . . "Who
> am I? What do I think? If I could say something to this person,
> what would I say if there were no strings attached, if there were
> no walls up? What would I say?" And that's just the beginning,
> just the seed of who they are gonna be when they become
> women. But you know, I know plenty of women who still
> haven't even gotten there. . . . So, finding your voice is getting an
> inkling and a seedling. It's a start in finding who you are, what
> makes you tick. And I think by playwriting, you write other
> people's stories or sometimes your story within other people's

story. It just starts the imagination. It starts the creative flow of stream of consciousness of characters. So many of these girls do tell parts of their story through these plays that they write. Some tell their whole story. You know at the beginning of this interview, you wanted a bit of my story, my history. That's the beginning of this energy. That was the start and we build [from] that. So maybe this is what we are doing with these girls.

Kaya's observations of girls were punctuated by a pattern she saw in women as well. She knew the work that she and fellow teaching artists asked the girls to do was hard and that teachers, too, were works in progress. For Kaya, it was being a woman that allowed her to see where the lives of teaching artists and student artists converged. Kaya named this convergence "the yearning for partnership," or companionship, that she saw as a consistent theme. Additionally it was the yearning for family and inclusion that helped her relate to incarcerated and formerly incarcerated girls:

And some of [the girls] didn't do something wrong, they were wronged. They were abandoned by their parents and they are now wards of the state. Some of [the girls] are in [detention centers] because of that. So I think that their voice is taken away when [they] are commanded all day and their voice is usually just flat out angry; therefore, it's a power struggle. But maybe by writing, girls can find more constructive ways of communication. And also by playwriting in pairs that we do . . . they learn so many things and so many skills about collaboration. Skills that they are gonna have to have later in life to hold a job, to hold a relationship, with a marriage or a partnership. So they have to collaborate. They have power struggles within the writing process. It's just like a little model of work outside of the facility, or work of any kind that involves relationship.

Since Kaya's primary responsibility was training and working with teaching artists, we talked at length about how she prepared for workshops. All teaching artists completed an evaluation of the workshops. Here, teaching artists were not only asked to describe "accomplishments" in the workshops but to describe "challenges as well." Teaching artists were also asked to describe suggestions for dealing with challenges—that Kaya took very seriously, as evidenced by her asking teaching artists to bring their expertise from other teaching experiences to improve Girl Time pedagogy. While Girl Time had a curriculum, Kaya encouraged flexibility to promote growth for both teaching artists and student artists:

> You know, there's a danger when you do something that works really well and you just keep doing that same thing. But I think that our teachers bring so many interesting skills that I'm really strong on listening to them and letting them have some owner-ship and letting them say, "I think this would be good here" and not just saying, "No that's not how we do it," hearing them out and letting them try their idea as much as possible so that we can continue to grow. And we don't have teachers in our ensemble just to dictate [to them] what to do, you know? It's an ensemble and teachers are a part of it. Teacher voices are important. If we are not honoring their voices as teachers, how can we then turn around and ask teachers to honor the girls' voices? So I try to talk myself through that before I get out of the car, "OK, why are we here? What are we doing? What is our mission? What is our goal? What is our greatest hope?" And then apply that to the teachers as well. I'm teaching the teachers and the teachers, including me, are teaching the girls. I want my body of teachers to continue to grow; therefore, they need to feel ownership.

Pre-meetings took place before every workshop for approximately a half an hour. What I found compelling about these meetings was that Kaya asked teaching artists to practice their verbiage for the activity or game they were scheduled to facilitate. I found out how daunting this could be during my first few workshops as a teaching artist; it was awk-ward to explain some of the physical warm-ups and games fluidly. Words did not always do justice to the physical movement. Yet as a former 1st-grade teacher, 10th-grade English teacher, and, currently, as a university professor, I understood how important it was to be prepared with how to communicate expectations clearly. In the Girl Time pre-meetings, teaching artists were able to receive feedback on their delivery while calling on the expertise of a team of fellow educators to support their efforts to commu-nicate effectively. Similar to my work with student poets and their team of teachers in the Power Writers in the Bronx (Fisher, 2005a, 2005b, 2007), I began to privilege the idea of teaching as a team as opposed to flying solo, trying to figure things out while isolated in your classroom. Kaya sup-ported the notion of an ensemble of teachers working together:

The really important thing is to go over the agenda so when we get in the detention center we can be a well-oiled machine and not just saying, "What's next? What's next?" Teachers have been emailed the agenda with their parts, their duties, but I like to talk through the flow. When I'm working with very new teachers I get them to vocalize how they are gonna do that or ask them specifically how they are gonna do that.

Ensemble was not a term that was on display; teachers worked toward this in all they touched. Playwriting and performance—and the girls experiencing success and accomplishment in these—began with teachers' preparation, "You have to build the trust. What makes an ensemble is that you trust each other. . . . I like to build trust in the teacher pre-meeting." Kaya opened pre-meetings by asking teaching artists questions such as, "Share one thing you created since we saw you," or "Tell us one beauty and one beast in your life right now." Creating ensemble was not without its drama. Welcoming tension to promote growth was a key component of teaching for social justice. How can teachers grow individually or as a team if they do not have the space to push or challenge each other? What if we do the same thing the same way just because we are comfortable even when students are not growing or developing?

The writing process began before girls received pencils and notepads. This was a strategic pedagogical strategy that Kaya referred to as "writing through the back door":

We don't just walk in there and say, "Here's a pencil." I think they'd freeze . . . A phrase I use when I'm teaching this work is, "You are coming in through the backdoor." Students don't even realize they're writing, instead they are learning to trust you. "Okay you are taking me somewhere. Okay I'm taking this first step with you. I'll write down different emotions. I'm on a deserted island, Okay I'll play this little game with you. Okay, this is kind of fun. Okay I'm warming up to this and I'm actually using a pencil and we're writing. Okay then you want me to write down relationship." So it's building, building, building the interests and building the ensemble. And then, the next thing you know, students create a beginning, middle, and end for their plays. We are not saying, "Now write." We've incorporated building the outline into it. So they're just coming in and they're like, "Oh wow, I've kind of got a play. I guess we just need to write the dialogue now." So we are bringing them in through the back door and making them comfortable. We are establishing trust. Part of the ensemble is, "Hey you're part of our family. Come play this game with us, do this with us, you know, pass the clap. Show us your name. Be proud of yourself." And they don't realize that they're trusting us, trusting each other, working as an ensemble, or they're working as a team. They do not even realize they're creating.

While a new observer in a Girl Time session might think time was being wasted, every sound, word, and movement is deliberate. Kaya and Anne created a method book; however, they were constantly revisiting it. Still, even when they revisited the curriculum, "writing through the back door" (Fisher, Purcell, & May, 2009) and "Yes, *and*" remained at the core of Girl Time's pedagogical practices:

It's so easy to negate. It's so easy. What we are doing through this writing process, theatre, acting, and creative process is showing [that] there really is no right or wrong. So we have to really be sensitive to that. "Yes, that's a great idea *and* then what? You need to build on it." If we know they can go further with it—"Okay [the character] is shooting at someone . . . you see that all the time, *and* what else is happening?" Or students will answer a question with "I like it because it's happy." "Yes, it's happy *and* what else is it?' It's just a way of encouraging them and then getting more from them while inviting them to think outside the box. You ask a question when you're teaching and you may have an answer in mind. But this is not arithmetic. There is not a formula to it. But if I'm trying to get them to go to a place . . . their answer is valid. Validate. Validate. Validate. Encourage. Encourage. Encourage. They are told in the facility, all day long, "No. No. No." "Shut up, you can't do that." "Shut up." "You have to do this; you can't do that." And in order to find their voice, you can't keep badgering it and cutting it down. I think you have to encourage, and the byproduct is self-respect, working as an ensemble and finding their voices.

"Completely Unqualified and Immensely Responsible": Anne

Anne was 5 years Kaya's junior and grew up in the northeast. "My home-town was a very, very White New England town with 5 minority kids, total, all adopted by White families." Anne had one older sister and two younger twin sisters. As the only "theatre person" in her family, Anne acknowledged her mother and father as "painters on the side" even though they were a dentist and an emergency room doctor, respectively. Anne's dark brown hair matched her eyes perfectly; she was always moving around and directing—something she did well. Even in the late stages of her first pregnancy she could not be still, and once her daughter was born she put her in a sling and kept on moving. Anne had the same level of energy when she carried her twins in the midst of a very hot summer program. While Kaya was born in the southeast and chose to return there to raise her family, Anne found herself in the southeast by default but quickly learned "artists can have a home and a life here," which was especially important for her as a director and for her husband, who was an actor. Our Place Theatre Company was founded by three women including Anne but was not initially conceptualized as woman-focused. Their first play, *The Feigned Courtesans* penned by Aphra Behn, celebrated the work of this woman playwright. After this successful production, Our Place continued its commitment to producing plays written by female playwrights as well as plays that had compelling roles for women.

A relatively young theatre company, Our Place received nonprofit status in 2000 and partnered with various women's organizations throughout the city, fighting domestic abuse and supporting women in other ways. If Our Place evolved organically, Girl Time was even more of a divine occurrence. It was the life of Prix, an African American girl coming of age in the Bronx against the backdrop of poverty, gang violence, abuse, and incarceration, that launched Girl Time. African American playwright, Kia Corthron, introduced the theatre world to Prix's world in the play *Breath, Boom* (2002). Prix's love of fireworks—the colors, beauty, and perceived freedom—largely symbolized her escape from her ongoing struggles to survive. Our Place produced Corthron's play with an ensemble of mostly Black women, "We wanted to treat the play very honestly," recalled Anne. While the cast shared the ethnicity of the girls in Corthron's play, they did not necessarily share their experiences of being in gangs or incarcerated. In order to understand what it would mean to live life in and out of jails and the prominence of gang activity in the lives of girls, the *Breath, Boom* cast organized an exchange of lived experiences, wisdom, and education with incarcerated girls who understood Prix and her peers. "We were scared by it. We were excited by it," Anne explained, "and that really convinced us that we should do more of it because it challenged us and because it mattered so much. It made sense that we should do more." In 2002, Girl Time was born and teaching artists conducted workshops in Main RYDC and eventually three more RYDCs outside the city limits.

Immediately Anne worried about the racial dynamics of the teaching ensemble. It would be, at best, irresponsible to ignore the fact that every detention center corralled a sea of black bodies and Anne wanted an ensemble of teaching artists with multiple ways of being in the world. Anne was hyperaware of her Whiteness, "I'm totally a White girl. I grew up in a White place without any diversity . . . I grew up with tremendous privilege and I have always really felt that means I have a huge responsibility. I feel both completely unqualified and immensely responsible to try to talk to and connect with these girls."

Anne's testimony of White privilege, power, and subsequent guilt is not an entirely new narrative especially when America's public school teaching force continues to consist of largely White middle-class women working with Black and Latino students. Anne's narrative, however, named her deeply rooted fear of being "discovered," that resonates with many educators of all backgrounds. "My biggest fear is the girls are going to know my secret, which is that I haven't had a hard life . . . What right do I have really? I don't know their life and they're going to know that."

Anne chose to listen and hear one of the early Girl Time collaborators. Through a partnership with an organization committed to teaching dance to urban inner city youth, Julienne, an African American woman, had the temerity to challenge Girl Time's and, specifically, Anne's self-image as a progressive educator. Julienne worked for Girl Time and helped Anne with preparing teachers to work in Girl Time's detention center workshops. Anne's initial approach with the girls was to coddle and encourage to the point that some girls attempted to shift the focus of the ensemble from working as a cohesive unit to being immersed in power struggles. "Julienne said she found it funny when she trained White teachers—and I haven't found a really good way to say this yet—but she said White teachers need to get in touch with their inner black momma who sometimes has to say, 'Listen, you need to get on your feet and do this now.'" For Anne, Julienne's observations made her more aware that each interaction and encounter with the girls required a nuanced response as opposed to adopting one chosen method that privileged Anne's experience only. "So that's been a lesson too and you know I've seen each of the sort of teachers come from a different experience . . . so we all have to kind of figure that out."

Anne had several stories about Girl Time; however, there was one experience that always stood out for her when trying to describe why she found playwriting and performance so important in the lives of girls:

> So this girl in the detention center comes running up to me, "Anne, Anne, Anne!" and she had this paper that was all rolled up, and she unrolled it and it was the script she'd written in our workshop 2 months earlier. It had clearly been rolled and unrolled over and over again. All I could think was, in the past 2 months I had directed a play, I'd been out to restaurants, I'd been hanging out with friends, living my life. And she'd been in there listening to that door slam over and over and over again and held on to this play. And it's not easy to hold on to stuff in there either. And so that meant so much to me because she cared enough to hold onto it and maybe, just maybe, it was something that helped her get through that time, because if you create something, you're worth something. If there's something that comes from your hands and your heart and your mind, it proves to you that you're worth something because you've made an impact. And you did it with your own smarts and your own heart and your own brain and your own imagination. And I think that the value of that cannot be underestimated.

"Little Black Girl": Zaire

One of Girl Time's first teachers, and one who had no problem accessing her "inner Black momma," was Zaire. Zaire auditioned for a part in *Breath, Boom*, but once Anne discovered she was a costume designer as well she enlisted her as the latter. A self-professed "little Black girl," Zaire announced she was "thirty-something" and that I better leave it at that. While her roots were in the heart of Texas, Zaire lived "damn near everywhere" including New York City, South Africa, West Africa, Florida, Ohio, and California. "My education background is in theatre and sociology," Zaire shared, "And interestingly enough [I studied] sociology because I like to watch people and theatre because it was my first love. But my mom was like, 'That's cute but what are you going to do for real?'" Her personality and audacity are encapsulated in a story she tells about her mother polling a young Zaire for destinations for their next vacation. "And I was like '[let's go to] Paris!' And my mom asked, 'Paris, Texas?' I said, 'No, the other one!' to which she replied, 'You're a little extravagant!'"

Zaire's identity was largely informed by what she was not. Her sister was the "all-American, light skinned, thin girl" who Zaire remembers everyone wanting to befriend. Zaire viewed herself as the "ugly duckling" next to her swan of a sister, "I was the little black girl. Back then it wasn't very popular to be the little black girl. And to be fat too! I wasn't very popular. And so you start thinking that all you are is the sum of your body parts and what you can offer and what people can take from you." Raised in a city suffocating from a heavy blanket of intense drug culture, and crack cocaine in particular, Zaire's hard-working mother tried to create an oasis for her girls by reminding them of their beauty and values. Zaire still retreated to a world where she felt like she fit in and learned that "people are more than the sum of the choices they make." Her spirit and creativity were unparalleled and Zaire's unwavering commitment to the girls was inspiring to the teaching artists and detention center staff. Zaire was an experience from her spiraled jet black dreadlocks (with one much longer than the others wrapped in metallic silver fabric dangling below her waist). She would not be caught dead without stilettos and nails painted with fantastical patterns channeling the late Olympian runner Florence Griffith-Joyner better known as "Flo Jo." When Zaire walked into the detention center she greeted the guards and personnel with a "Hey, baby" and they responded with big smiles and hugs. Girls in the detention center reached out to touch her as if they could not believe she was real or as if they had just seen their very own fairy godmother.

Zaire's belief in her work with Girl Time and incarcerated youth was embedded in the ways in which singing, acting, and performing, in general, gave a "little black girl" a place to shine, stand out, and be acknowledged. If both Kaya and Anne viewed their upbringing and lives in contrast to youth in underserved schools and communities, Zaire viewed her lived experiences as parallel to incarcerated and formerly incarcerated girls. Zaire's declaration, "I'm a little Black girl," a title she continued to claim in spite of earning a bachelor's and two master's degrees, was her point of convergence with the girls she sought to serve. Zaire believed that not much separated her from the girls; at one point in her life she found herself in a courtroom awaiting a judge's decision about her fate after getting involved in illegal activities. When she was given a second chance by the judge and jury; she did not take it lightly. Zaire counted herself among the lucky ones, especially in a "global lockdown" climate for women of color (Sudbury, 2005). In 2008, Black women reached the "1 in 100" mark for America's incarcerated (Pew Center on the States, 2008) and Zaire knew she could have been among them.

Zaire's lived experiences—especially using theatre and drama as a tool—influenced her teaching especially when it came to encouraging girls to understand their worth:

> When I lead the circles, I do this thing where we stand in a circle and I [say], "Turn to the person to your left and tell them something that you like about them. Not their shoes, not their shirt, not their hair. Tell them something that you like or appreciate about them that is not visible." Now this is the interesting thing about that. Somebody will be like, "Well it's easy for the teachers [to do this] because we are in tune [with each other]." But the issue is that one girl can turn to another girl and the first thing they do is they start giggling because they're uncomfortable. They fidget and giggle. And when the other girl says something to them, they don't look them in the eye. Now if the girl said [something negative] to the other girl she would respond and go off, etc. . . . So I ask, "but now that she says something that lifts your spirit, why don't you think you deserve to hear that? Why don't you think that's just as valid as everything else?" And instead of you shrugging it off, say, "Thank you." Take it. Receive it. Own it. Let that feeling roll through you for a while because a lot of times we feel bad about feeling good about ourselves. A lot of times it's just so much easier to believe the negative shit, especially for girls. There are not a lot of people telling girls great stuff that they wanna remember.

When Zaire was asked to define her role as a teacher, she summed it up in five words, "I am a seed planter." Indeed, Zaire consistently planted these small and curious seeds that were a synthesis of ideas and methods from not only her theatre background but also her work in sex and sexuality education with girls and women who were either HIV positive or living with AIDS:

> I'm a seed planter. I plant seeds. Because you know what? You may not hear something I said today. But when you really need it, you're gonna remember something I say. Because a lot of times, people hear you but they don't listen because they can't listen. Because it's not time for them to listen. It's not time for

them to really hear it. So, you know, that's just what I do. I wanna plant seeds.

Zaire was also a teacher of the teachers. Girl Time stretched me as a teacher more than I could imagine. I created this false reality that in order to work in this context I had to be completely together every single day; I felt tremendous pressure to show the girls a polished side. When I mentioned this to Zaire on a day when I did not feel particularly bright and shiny, she gave me one of her loving rants: "You don't teach nobody nothing by being perfect every day. All you do when you try to be perfect every day is show these girls something that they can't be. Be real. They have to know we have real stuff going on in our lives too but it doesn't stop us from wanting to be here with them and our fellow teachers. You have to show them that we got to keep moving." We just stared at each other and then both started laughing. "Damn, that was good, wasn't it?" Zaire complimented herself. "It really was!" I replied still amused at how she could just spew wisdom from her fountain so quickly. "Now you need to put that in that damn book!" Zaire ordered.

"As Long as I Wasn't the Star": Carrie Mae

Born in 1960 in Germany to an African American military family, Carrie Mae's parents settled with their son and two daughters in the southeastern United States. As the baby in her family, Carrie Mae was the most seasoned woman in the Girl Time teaching ensemble, but her energy and consistent enthusiasm were abundant. The only thing that hinted that Carrie Mae was older than the other teachers was the silver streak in an otherwise coal black sea of wavy hair. Hoping their daughter would have a job with a "steady income or pension" Carrie Mae's parents recognized how happy she was acting. She enjoyed a recurring role on a television sitcom, as well as other theatre work and many teaching jobs outside of Girl Time. "When I hear my mother talking to my nieces and nephews she says, 'Look at Aunt Carrie . . . She's poor as a mouse but she is happy!'" After completing college at a research university and studying theatre, Carrie Mae made plans to move to New York City and become a "Black Sally Field." Sally Field, according to Carrie Mae, was the consummate supporting actress. "As long as I wasn't the star," explained Carrie Mae, "then I could always have something to strive for." She stayed in the southeast and became a resident of a thriving theatre company for 5 years, did a 4-year stint in New York City, and returned to a productive acting career in the southeast including a one-woman play she wrote about African American women activists. Among the African American women Carrie Mae played were Bessie Coleman, Harriet Tubman, Barbara Jordan, Stagecoach Mary, Ida B. Wells, Wilma Rudolph, and Edmonia Lewis. This one-woman show was available for public school performances. Carrie Mae worked with youth in other capacities as well. One of the theatre companies Carrie Mae worked with hosted a weekend science academy for youth, "I saw children come alive with an understanding of math and science in very slight ways . . . but just the fact that they were thinking . . . and there were kids who may not have enjoyed science are now acting out science scenes and doing research . . . asking questions. And so I learned about a power of theatre that I hadn't understood before."

Carrie Mae's predictable military-base life contrasted greatly with the lives of girls who participated in Girl Time's workshops. Prior to working with the girls, Carrie Mae taught ensemble building and acting techniques to incarcerated women who, with the help of a resident playwright, developed shows:

> It was such an eye-opening experience for me. First of all it was my first time thinking about these women as women and not as prisoners, not as a menace to society but real people with real feelings. And maybe they made a mistake . . . but they are people and they still cry at night when no one is looking and they still get overjoyed when they get a piece of gum.

Like many teachers who find themselves generations removed from the students they teach, Carrie Mae had questions about the girls in front of her, "Who are these girls? What's going on in their world today that I'm not a part of because I'm in my late 40s, so I ask what don't I know about 13-year-old girls. What are they experiencing? What the girls experience is a different kind of education even if it's not formally recognized in schools."

Channeling Freire, Carrie Mae knew that she had to learn about her students' worlds and release her own educational experiences as the sole source of knowledge. Like Zaire, Carrie Mae's desire and intention was to meet the girls where they were, even if it meant suppressing her inclination to critique; "Because no matter how facilitative I think I am, there's a part of me that is still very much a mother—even though I don't have children—that wants to shake my finger and tell them how to do things and just make their lives easier for them so it won't be so bad . . . I constantly fight with telling them what to do and trying to let them come to it on their own accord." Carrie Mae's desire to shake her finger at the girls was an honest portrayal of how educators can feel at various points in their teaching journey. There have been workshops in which the teaching ensemble had to check in with each other or depend on each other for patience. Carrie Mae appreciated the simple question Kaya asked to bring everyone back together during points of frustration, "Ask yourselves why are you here?"

Working as an ensemble or as a team was one of Girl Time's greatest strengths. The more work I did with community-based organizations that promoted coalition building, the more convinced I became that it is unfair and unwise to teach alone. At some of the small schools where I work, teachers meet in grade-level teams, which is a first and critical step to supporting students and teachers. Carrie Mae credited teaching as a team for the impact Girl Time made with student artists:

> I think it's interesting because not everyone can work in teams. Sometimes people are trying to show off their own skills, and I think it takes a real ability to gather women together with various strengths who don't mind other people showing their strengths. And if I'm working with the girl and I'm getting impatient, depending on . . . the type of tension that has occurred, I might call forth Zaire who has a very strong motherly [instinct], "You're gonna do that kind of thing" to talk to some of the girls, or I might have them talk to Kaya who has that like, You can do it vibe. So it's really nice to not have to be on your own. . . . Sometimes it takes two teachers together. And it's nice because you don't have all the pressure on your shoulders; you've got somebody else who you know is really good with movement and you can ask what you should do in a certain case. I don't have to succeed on my own.

"Standing for What's Best in Them": Petulia

Carrie Mae worked with another teaching artist, Petulia, in other theatre companies. It was not unusual for Petulia and Carrie Mae to carpool together and spend time beyond the Girl Time workshops. Born in 1972 in a suburban area of Ohio, Petulia described herself as a "mutt": "I mean there are many—English, Irish, Welsh, Native American, a little bit of African American, and I don't know what else. Those are the ones I know."

If one were to question Petulia's ethnicity they might comfortably come to the conclusion that she was White. With her face always framed by a stylish haircut and smart looking glasses, Petulia's smile was consistent and her outlook always positive. Her gift for getting into character and staying there while everyone around her was delirious with laughter added a new dimension to the notion of "committing" in theatre. Petulia grew up with her parents and one older sister in the Midwest. She earned a Bachelor in Arts in acting in her home state before moving to the southeast in her early 20s. An ordained minister—something that I never knew until I interviewed her—who took pride in officiating ceremonies that were "nontraditional" including commitment ceremonies, Petulia taught theatre in a variety of settings. "So I actually do feel like the theatre and ministry intertwines. How do you open toward people and close toward people? Really looking a lot within yourself. How do you open yourself to a connection?"

Petulia's teaching experience prior to Girl Time was extensive and she gave a great deal of thought to using theatre as a tool for rebuilding relationships with the self and others. After the disturbing shootings at Columbine High School in Colorado, Petulia worked with a theatre company that confronted the notion of bullying and violence. Additionally, this theatre company, much like Our Place, wanted to use theatre to foster community dialogue. "Frank Wittow's idea was what if you brought theatre exercises into the schools, into the classrooms, and started breaking down barriers—you know where you've got all the cliques happening and it really starts happening in middle school." Carrie Mae was already involved in Wittow's project when Petulia joined the ensemble. Both teaching artists believed in Wittow's vision that building ensemble with students and teachers could facilitate communication and community building. Initially the classroom teachers they worked with believed they were "really busy and really too stressed" to even consider theatre. Through an intense collaboration the team of teaching artists and the classroom teachers discovered "it's worthwhile to spend ten minutes a day doing something that's ensemble building because kids learned to work together," and it meant stronger connections throughout the academic year. Carrie Mae asked Petulia to consider working with Girl Time.

"I see my role as an encourager," Petulia said of working with incarcerated and formerly incarcerated girls, "[I am] someone who is taking a stand for them . . . who is pushing them a little bit and believing in them. [I am] someone who's standing for what's best in them or believing in the goodness in them. And so we're introducing this tool. I'm introducing this tool of theatre, writing, of expression."

Again, the notion of deservingness or worthiness and helping youth discover that they are both deserving and worthy was central to Petulia's work with the girls. Petulia's prior work influenced her teaching philosophy:

> Frank from the Academy always trained us in the basic psychological needs of children and one of them was to feel "good" at something, another one was to feel important to someone. So I feel like if we can give them just a little bit of feeling important and successful at something, that's just like a drop in the bucket of a life experience.

Petulia used this as a foundation for working with girls during the playwriting process. She was decidedly "hands off" when it came to the girls composing their plays. "Even if it's a story I've heard a hundred times before," explained Petulia," I think it's up to them to say the kind of story they want." Petulia was also a part of launching Girl Time's after school program for upper elementary and middle school girls. In an effort to disrupt the school-to-prison pipeline, Girl Time teaching artists often imagined a program for girls who had not experienced the juvenile justice system. Petulia, at the time a mother of one, believed in the power of introducing theatre early in girls' lives. Kaya, Petulia, Mindy, and I piloted the first after school program in the fall of 2006. For 6 weeks we were able to work with an ensemble of girls twice a week for 4-hour blocks. These imagination and creativity workshops blended all of the techniques that Kaya, Petulia, and Mindy studied over the years. While I did not include the after school program as part of this study, the experience informed our work with formerly incarcerated girls:

> I loved having so much time with the girls. Personally, I loved having a chance to help create the curriculum and help craft the program because it was a much smaller group of us. And being engaged with the girls over a longer period of time you would start to see where each one needed to grow. And because we had formed that relationship with them, we could more effectively call them on their specific things. Work with them over time to get clear and less fidgety. You could just engage on a different l evel because you had a chance to see them every week. It was also so nice to see the ensemble really grow with them. I felt like we could keep coming back to that and keep growing that over time.

Petulia found the extended period of time with girls to be a creative nest for teachers and it gave her a dynamic perspective of the work. Looking at the work across a trajectory—first, with upper elementary and junior high school girls at the age that many of the Girl Time student artists cited as their most difficult time, then with girls who experienced incarceration, and finally with girls who were released—invited teaching artists to continue their growth and development.

"Theatre Is What Held It Together for Me": Isis

Girl Time's teaching ensemble was a microcosm of the close-knit theatre and activist community in this urban southeastern city. While working for a nonprofit organization focused on preventing the transmission of HIV with a focus on African American women, Isis met Zaire, who told her about Girl Time. Born in 1980 to a mother who was an aspiring attorney and a father who was an ex-Black Panther, Isis was born in Madison, Wisconsin. After her parents divorced, Isis' mother moved her family to Washington, D.C., so she could finish her law degree and, eventually, to the San Francisco Bay Area:

> And that's where most of my childhood happened, in California—in the Bay Area. [I] went to mostly private schools— lots of different schools. [I] just kind of got bounced around . . . a lot of it was because of financial reasons. There were times when we were on welfare, but my mom was still keeping me in private school. That was a struggle but I give thanks to her for that.

As Isis "bounced around" from one private school to another following the ebbs and flows of her mother's financial situation, education remained her mother's priority. However in her mother's determination to make sure Isis had access to what she viewed as the best education, Isis found herself the only Black child in her classes and "constantly challenging racism." Isis developed a critical lens at a young age, "Either I was challenging racism or shrinking to it. There was always that balance that I still deal with in my life now. I don't always want to be the angry Black woman but I don't want to be dominated or a victim of oppression either." It was evident that Isis wanted the girls in the youth detention centers that housed Girl Time workshops to resist domination and oppression as well. Always wearing a touch of the color purple—her favorite color—whether it be the carefully chosen purple-kissed dreadlocks peaking from behind the other mostly brown locks or the tattoo of the continent of Africa evenly colored in red, black, and green, or a t-shirt with an affirming message, Isis embodied Black liberation, which she studied at the university. "I enrolled in California State Long Beach in the Black Studies [program] and worked with Dr. Maulana Karenga, the founder of Kwanzaa.[2] And it was really a life-changing thing because I was at the point where I really wanted to be about African liberation but also my liberation as a woman." Eager to explore African liberation through a womanist and feminist lens, Isis was reluctant to continue the program, which she found to be male-dominated and a bit stifling. Having recently left an abusive marriage and raising a daughter, Isis moved to the urban southeast to study in a program at a Historically Black College/University (HBCU) that supported her vision.

Theatre was always a part of Isis' life and, like Zaire, performance became her opportunity to be seen and heard when she felt invisible and voiceless. In her teenage years, Isis became involved in an East Oakland gang affiliated with the Crips. Isis decided she was tired of being called "dirty," and "poor," and other names by other girls in her Catholic school. The name-calling was exacerbated by the fact that Isis was the only student who had to ride the bus, meaning she did not participate in the elaborate and cliquish carpool system in which many students and parents bonded. "So I hooked up with this gang and they gave me an unloaded gun to take to school with me for protection. Just to scare people . . . It was one of those places where I was on a path where I could end up being locked up." Ironically Isis was privileged when compared to her peers who were in a gang, yet, in her school community she was so isolated that she identified more with young people who had already been pushed out of school.

"When I was at that fork [in the road]," explained Isis, "and could join the gang or stay focused on something that was really going to help me in life, theatre is what held it together for me. Being able to go and perform where voice and expression [made me feel] like I could just lose myself in the story and become someone else. And the motivation to be a part of that—to be a part of a theatre company kept me off the streets." While Zaire and Isis had very different life experiences, both teachers believed they could have been one of the girls. "When I read about Girl Time," Isis explained, "I said, 'I have to do this program because this is me.' This is me and I had this overwhelming desire to meet these young ladies and provide some type of guidance based on my experience. So I called Zaire to talk about it, met with Anne and they invited me."

Isis' teaching style was an extension of her work in the world; she was observant, listened intensely before speaking, and worked hard at finding the best in every situation. When she walked into a workshop she took the temperature of the room:

> I see [my role] as just kind of stepping back and feeling the
> energy in the room. I try to connect with the sisters who are
> there, just one-on-one, as much as possible I get a feel for their
> energy and what they're bringing into the room and just sort of
> taking a step back, leaving whatever I'm dealing with outside
> so that I can be there for them, and just absorb and connect with
> whatever it is that they're dealing with in a way that affirms
> them and validates their experience. I think what happens a lot
> in the juvenile justice system is their experience is completely
> disregarded. Their feelings, their emotions, are completely disre-
> garded. They aren't looked at as individuals or as people, but as
> inmates or some type of thing that is possessed but not appreci-
> ated or accepted. So I feel like part of my role there is to reaffirm
> the human dignity of their existence by providing a space for
> them to have voice and to voice that they are and to help them
> find that voice.

Similar to Petulia, Isis saw her role as affirming "human dignity" and "voice." The pedagogy of playwriting and performing—as opposed to writing poems, stories, and other prose—was essential to this process according to Isis. Other forms of writing could be too singular, whereas, plays demanded dialogue and considering multiple perspectives:

> Playwriting I think is a different way of telling a story. I mean, to
> me, the power of being able to tell your story or to tell a story—
> most of the stories that the young ladies write are based on their
> own lives or on the lives of people that they've been intimately
> connected with—so the power of being able to tell those stories,
> I think that's where the playwriting aspects come in. And play-
> writing is so great because everyone that comes into the story,
> [they] have their own voice within the story. So it sort of vali-
> dates those stories from the different perspectives of the people
> involved. . . . And it challenges them to consider all of the play-
> ers, all of the characters . . . keeps this sense of integrity of the
> relationships between the characters.

"I Was the Identifier": Mindy

While the White teaching artists in Girl Time overwhelmingly approached their work with incarcerated and formerly incarcerated girls from a need to balance their sense of privilege, Black teaching artists approached their work from what Isis characterized as the "this is me" perspective. Actress, comedian, and talk show host Mo'nique titled her performance in a women's correctional facility in Ohio as "I Coulda' Been Your Cell Mate . . . ," underscoring the thin line between all Black women's lives in a country eager to incarcerate them and throw away the key. Mindy, a Girl Time teaching artist, named this difference: "I find this so interesting that the difference between the White and Black teachers—from what I understand Anne's impetus for this work is—'I've never been there but I want to give back because I've always had so much I want to give to those who never have.' I'm saying, 'Oh, I've been there and I understand this.'" Born in 1976 outside Baltimore, Maryland, into an "upwardly mobile Black middle class family," Mindy considered herself to be the "identifier" in an abusive family masked by a two-parent and two-salary household in which she and her brother had all the material things they needed. "My household was very much one of secrets—one of denial. I was the identifier or the only one whose behavior wasn't saying 'everything is hunkydory' . . . When I had the opportunity to leave I did so." Mindy went to study musical theatre at a northeastern university. After 2.5 years she left the program and moved to the urban southeast where she trained with a theatre company that worked with youth. "I was trained to be a play creator, and spent a summer workshop paired with a worker at a local residential youth psychiatric facility using multiple artistic disciplines to help the youth create an original work based on their experiences titled, "If You Only Knew."

Mindy did a show with Our Place—that's when she first heard Anne talking about Girl Time. At that point Girl Time was less than 1-year old with only two workshops under its belt, and Mindy wanted to continue the kind of work she had done in the residential youth psychiatric program. "In my previous work I posed this question to kids, 'What is the one thing that if people knew about you, they would understand you better?' I thought that being on stage and performing was the only thing I could do to be happy. But to see [the girls] grow and develop and just take that much ownership in themselves was phenomenal."

Mindy hardly missed a workshop, "I think I have missed a total of two workshops . . . I am always available . . . If I can find a way to be there

I am going to be there. It nourishes me." Not only did Mindy teach in the detention center workshops and the summer program (including serving as the music director for the opening act), she also taught in the inaugural Girl Time after school program created to disrupt the school-to-prison pipeline. The after school program—just one of the programs that was developed during the tenure of my study—was focused on middle school girls. Mindy saw similarities in Girl Time's work across contexts:

> I think anytime you have a chance to tell a child that they are worth something, that their voice is worth something, and that people are here to listen and that people want to hear, it is a good thing. I think that the more encouragement you can give children, the better. The ability to give them encouragement. When we say to them, "This does not have to end here. You can write at any time. You can create at any time. Please continue to do so. Look at what you did in just 2 days. With limited time, limited resources look at what you can do. All you need is paper and a pen. And you don't even need that if you just create it organically" . . . and being able to show them that. That they can continue to create. When we get a break and we get to talk to them, it's just amazing the amount of kids who [tell us], "Oh, I've already written three plays," "Oh, I have a whole notebook of poetry," "Oh, I rap." And sometimes you'll find that the next day, they'll bring it in to show it to you. Encouraging them in that, to express themselves in a positive way, in a nonviolent way, can make a big difference.

Mindy learned that Girl Time student artists were not creating for the first time when they wrote plays or refined characters for the program, which is an idea I explore further in the fifth and final act. Girls came with journals, notebooks, little pieces of paper, and in some cases a draft of a memoir or autobiography. This was revealed during the summer program; it was not unusual to have girls present a body of work at the end of the week after getting to know teachers and fellow student artists. For many of the girls it was a revelation to have a community of people interested in their creations, and they felt safe revealing their work. In much of the work, girls named the issues that disrupted their lives. Mindy explained:

> One of the things I love the most about our work, especially in the detention centers, but in Girl Time in general, is that outside

of profanity, we do not censor them. These children are constantly being told what they can and cannot do, and what they
can and cannot say . . . and to respect their elders no matter what
. . . to respect authority no matter what without having any sense
of [how] respect [is defined]. To give them an opportunity to
show authority as they see it or to tell adults what they believe
makes a good parent . . . to show a police system [that] may take
advantage . . . to show a society that takes advantage of youth, of
innocence. To highlight the circumstances that led them to where
they are. Because often these children are nothing but the identi-
fiers, just like I was. They're constantly being told, "You have
issues." [Authorities] say, "This child is a runaway, lock her up,"
[without] addressing why the child ran away. And all of a sud-
den [girls] are branded. To have the opportunity to say to these
children, "What do you have to say? Just talk to us and we're not
gonna judge you." We have times when we do the session and
we come out of there and we have nothing but guns, shootings,
and suicide in the plays, and it breaks our heart every time, but
we don't censor it. We never say, "Can we just make this a happy
ending? Can we just tie this up in a pretty bow?" Because that's
not life, and that's not their experience. And we are there for
them to tell their story.

"Drama Brat": Ginger

"I'm a Christmas baby," explained Ginger, "I was born the day after
Christmas." Born in a small town that lost its economic base when a
major corporation closed its doors, Ginger moved to a "big city" in the
southeast when she was 10. "It was a really sad town," Ginger said of
her birthplace; however, her family had resources and were able to relo-
cate. Theatre, according to Ginger was "always, always, always" a part
of her life although she took a hiatus from it when she got to high school
before returning to the stage at age 22. Adding "nontraditional theatre"
to her trajectory, Ginger started emceeing and participating in what she
referred to as "street theatre." "For me [theatre] comes in a performance
aspect . . . no matter what it is I've always had a drive to perform." A
self-proclaimed "drama brat," Ginger's mother and cousin were also involved in theatre.

Ginger was spunky. She spoke with a sweet voice but could be
tough when she wanted to. Ginger waited tables at a popular eatery;

however, once it "sold out" and became "too corporate" she found another mom-and-pop restaurant where she could get to know her customers. She learned about Girl Time through her internship at Our Place in 2003. When Anne described the Girl Time program, Ginger "thought it was genius and really wanted to be a part of it."

Ginger defined herself as queer and found Our Place and Girl Time a safe space to be herself as a teacher:

> I think this program enables us to connect in a whole new way
> . . . I have friends who are teachers in traditional school settings.
> They are lesbians but they are not allowed to be out. They aren't
> allowed to discuss it. And they have students who have just
> come out, and they are facing all this stuff with their peers but
> aren't allowed to talk to them about it.

Ginger and Isis participated in a street performance reenacting the notorious Stonewall incident for a local "Pride" festival in 2007. "Stonewall was a bar in the sixties that was a gay bar," explained Ginger, "and it was raided and a riot ensued and it sort of marked the gay movement. And so this group got some people together to reenact sort of what happened at Stonewall." During breaks in the Girl Time summer program in 2007, girls got to watch Ginger and Isis rehearse their lines of poetry and prose for this project. Witnessing the continuum of theatre and performance in the teaching artists' lives demonstrated the multiple ways these teachers were present in the world:

> I think a lot of the teachers have had different experiences, and
> we come together because we have this one interest of theatre
> and performance. We like to share that. And we're also interested
> in these young women and sharing that with them. And I think
> it's great. It's sort of like . . . an interest in all sort of walks of life.
> We are diverse enough that there is someone who's had an ex-
> perience that is relatable . . . I do think it's great that I identify as
> queer. If when we work with the young women who also iden-
> tify as queer, it's great to have an older person to represent it. It
> definitely, you know, makes them feel included and as if they can
> relate.

In some ways Ginger's life mirrored the girls' lives more than most Girl Time teaching artists. Like Zaire, and Isis, Ginger found art to be a tool for healing especially after experiencing some setbacks during her teenage years. "I definitely connected with [the girls] from a personal level," Ginger offered. "Being a teenager that had gotten in a lot of trouble . . . I know for me, artistic endeavors have been so important to me personally in my recovery and healing from the kind of trouble I used to get into." Ginger described her background as "privileged"; her family was Caucasian, upper middle class, and "could afford private school." Ginger had never been sent to a detention center while a youth; however, she considered her teen years "more or less institutionalized." According to Ginger the difference between her and the girls she worked with in Girl Time was access to resources:

> My family was basically able to afford to keep me out of the juvenile detention system . . . Some of these issues we hear from the young women [about] why they're in the detention . . . like, "Ok, I ran away from home." Not only does that bring up all kind of [questions] like, why did you run away from home? [but] why are you in jail for that? I also connect deeply with that because it was one of the things I did . . . from drugs, to getting kicked out of school, skipping school, all that kind of stuff. I definitely think I would have gone to a detention center at some point during all of that. And the only reason I didn't was that my mom would sort of circumvent it by moving me to a different school or putting me somewhere else so I was in a safe space, so that I couldn't get in trouble. So I definitely just relate to the things that they do . . . because I did that myself. [It] was sort of illuminating for me to see, like "We did the same thing," and yet a kid like me, didn't end up in juvenile. I went to prep school kind of thing. And that's how it was addressed in my life. So [they are] the same exact problems, and they're just completely different as far as how they're dealt with and how they adjust.

Ginger named the class difference; her family could afford to send her to private schools that "dealt with these behaviors," whereas parents and guardians of the girls in Girl Time did not always have the resources to get their children out of the system. Countless mothers appealed to us that their daughters started in gifted programs, did all of their homework, and everything seemed to be fine. But one day something happened—a boy, the wrong crowd, the mother was working all the time or it became difficult to communicate. And the next thing they knew they received a call from a facility informing them that their child was being detained. There were never calls from school or administrators offering interventions. For other parents and guardians the system was a living breathing creature, an unavoidable noose around their necks or the necks of their loved ones. Some families were always in the system as were the people around them and unable to circumvent it the way Ginger's mother was. Sometimes the "system" was used to replace a father or a disciplinarian, and mothers committed their daughters to the system. However, Ginger's family, and mother in particular, found ways to get Ginger out of trouble. "[My mom] could go [to school] and talk to the teacher and explain, 'Oh this child is really gifted; she just has a problem . . . don't let her fail 9th grade, she needs to continue on. Look at her test scores. She's smart. She just has a problem.'" While Ginger named class and privilege, she did not name race. I asked her if she thought race played a role. "I do," Ginger eagerly responded. However, it was harder for her to analyze it the same way she was able to name class. I assured her we were all struggling to find the right language for all of this. Ginger explained:

> I just know my family had a lot of influence . . . especially my mom. Maybe that's because they're White, because they're educated. I think that kept me out of a lot of stuff. But I definitely think race had an impact. [The girls we work with] and their families are marginalized. They're pushed to the side as sort of . . . I don't know what the word is—it's that—like my experience getting reprimanded at school was . . . never like, "We are going to officially expel you or call the police." It was more like, "Call your parents." For the exact same things. And I really think money and race had a lot to do with those policies. Now why and how and how that all relates, I don't know. A lot of [the girls] have talked about how their parents, and especially their moms, and their families work a lot. And I mean if you're working two jobs, you can't run down to the school every other day and say, "You can't suspend my kid for this, she needs to be in classes" or "You can't expel her and this is what needs to happen." You can't have that kind of thing if you're working two jobs. You can't afford that kind of luxury. And that's part of how people get into the [detention] system.[3]

While I will offer an analysis of school-to-prison pipeline and the culture of zero-tolerance and surveillance in urban public schools later in Act

IV, Ginger raised an important point about the difference between the way her problems as a teenager were handled and those of the girls in the Girl Time program. Every effort was made to keep Ginger's record clean and avoid a paper trail that would label her and follow her throughout her life. All of Ginger's experiences shaped her as a teacher; she worked both from and through her experiences. Learning about Ginger's experiences also helped me understand what I came to call the "rearview mirror theory." When Girl Time conducted RYDC workshops, there were a few White girls in Main and many more in the detention centers located outside the city. However, none of the White girls ever continued their participation in the Girl Time summer program. Once after an RYDC workshop, I spoke to the father of one of our White participants. He explained to me, "This is just a blip on the screen for our daughter. We are going to put this in our rearview mirror and keep driving away until we cannot see it anymore." His confidence that it was possible to forget this incident in his daughter's life was unwavering, and it was clear he would do all he could to see to it that she was not in this situation again. Ginger's family had the same attitude and had the social and cultural capital to ensure that this was temporary, fleeting, and would not prohibit her from completing her schooling or anything else she wanted to do in life.

Ginger's narrative was also instrumental in helping me think about the unofficial teaching and learning spaces in the Girl Time program. During rides from the summer program to the train station, picking up and dropping girls off at home, and dinner and snack breaks, teaching artists reported illuminating discussions and experiences that brought them closer to the girls and to each other as a teaching team. Ginger named unofficial time "downtime" and she used this term consistently throughout her interview. Ginger's term downtime became one of my coding terms and helped me as I returned to sift through transcripts and field notes to name this important opportunity for interaction:

> I think it's important that we have some downtime during the program and we're able to have the conversations one-on-one with the girls. For instance, I drove one girl home one night, and she lived kind of far away so we were in the car for 30 minutes. And we had just a great discussion about all kinds of things, our past, our present, our hopes, and goals for the future. And those are the moments where we really get to connect, and get to share something intimate about ourselves. And it was really great, just to be given the opportunity to say, "This is what I did, and I

have been to jail, and this is what it's like." And she laughed and agreed. And I'm thinking that's part of my story and part of my past. So yeah, I mean I like the work [we] do and I think some other important work also happens when we have the down-time.

Ginger saw her role as a teacher as having a "strong presence" and to be "another person whose excited about being there and who's really into the work we're doing." Like many of the Girl Time teaching artists' pedagogical portraits, Ginger assumed a relationship between girls developing self-esteem and their ability to create something on their own:

> [Playwriting and performance] majorly affects self esteem and these [girls] have made this entire play from start to finish. And even if the actors who are in the play have not officially written that piece, they know one of their peers have. And I think, personally, it not only affects self-esteem, but it touches that place inside of all of us that longs to create and longs to express. And this is that opportunity for them. And in our school system right now, the arts are being cut from a lot of public schools.

"Theatre Is Like a Free Thing": Julisa

After performing in an Our Place play, Julisa learned about Girl Time. She reached out to Anne, interviewed, and joined the teaching-artist ensemble. "When I read about the program, I thought, this is extremely interesting because you know, it wasn't then I felt like I identified with the girls, but it was just like putting theatre into a place where, you know, they are still confined in so many ways and theatre is like a free thing." Julisa became a core teaching artist quickly because she hardly ever missed a workshop and was also able to teach during the summer program. She learned the teaching artist verbiage and facilitated many of the warm-ups and games. Julisa recalled her first Girl Time RYDC workshop:

> My first experience I was totally heartbroken. I went home and I just cried. I was upset that the girls were like behind bars and I just felt like jail wasn't the place for them because they were so bright, they were so intelligent and are capable of doing so much. Many of the girls were articulate and could speak about anything. In my first [workshop] the girls wrote a play that had

a talking dog? You're incarcerated and writing about a talking dog. Are you serious? [Girl Time] took them to a playful place . . . they may not get to see that all the time. I don't know if it was like the life-changing experience, I know it did something to me to go in and see that. It made me feel like I wasn't doing enough in life for myself or for anybody else.

Julisa was incredibly tall; while her height certainly gave her presence, her warmth and accessibility gave her even more. She was graceful and totally comfortable in her body. Later I learned she was a dancer as well as an actor, which explained her grace and fluidity of movement. Julisa launched into a discussion of what Girl Time meant for her as a teaching artist:

It's like it's bringing in a sense of doing something outside of the reality of the world that you're in. I feel sometimes that's what we need. They get stuck on our reality that we aren't able to see what's actually happening. We get stuck on what we feel is our reality so we need to be showed something outside of the box.

Julisa did not talk much about her life growing up, but she identified herself as African American and grew up in a close-knit family in the southeast. Throughout the interview, Julisa reflected on how much the girls transformed her and especially how they complicated her "single story" of incarcerated youth, "[My consciousness] definitely, I think, evolved over the process," Julisa began thoughtfully. After pausing, she continued:

What happened was I started seeing myself in a lot of the girls and I started seeing areas where I had problems when I was younger or where my sisters and I have problems. And I realized the only difference between us and them is that something happened where something got lost along the way where they didn't get the support they needed. Whereas my sisters and I— we had all kinds of [support]. But I just looked at [the girls] and just saw how much they were like me and it just made me want to do better.

As a single-mother to one son, Julisa juggled work, child care, acting, and dancing. She was incredibly forthcoming about her process of learning to embrace the girls in the program and exemplified how much Girl Time was not solely focused on transforming the girls but transforming the lives of those witnessing, involved in the teaching. "A lot of times I saw the bias I developed toward the girls who are actually just like me," confessed Julisa:

> I'm really thankful for the Girl Time program because a lot of
> times it shows me the bias that I developed towards girls that
> are actually just like me. And it's not that I wanted to use biases,
> but somehow along the line I have developed it. And it helps me
> to fight those biases because I recognize them as someone like
> myself, or not like myself, but someone who can or, if given the
> right opportunities, can do something great.

Julisa carried some powerful ideas about theatre as a kind of voicing to her work with Girl Time, "I think it's a chance to voice anything that I want to voice and you know I'm not offending anybody because in theatre you don't take it so wholeheartedly . . . you take it as a performance and you take it and you look at it like you know that was a performance that I can maybe apply it to my real life. But you're not taking it like you would take something like criticism or something." Like Kaya, Julisa emphasized the compelling nature of voice; however, for Julisa her work was about showing the girls they have a voice rather than thinking she was giving them voice. "I think I'm responsible for showing the girls that they have a voice and options" offered Julisa, "and there is a strength in you that sometimes you don't recognize."

Teaching these elements of Girl Time curriculum really took place in the doing. Julisa often acted side-by-side with the girls. Kaya recognized Julisa's ability to commit to her characters and saw how much the girls got focused after observing Julisa. One time Kaya cast me as Monica in "Ghosts of the Past," and Julisa played Monica's fiancé, Robert. Julisa was so good that I was absolutely paralyzed and we always had a good laugh remembering how I fell into her arms at the end of the play:

> [Theatre] is a nontraditional form of teaching. Traditionally you
> have to tell [students], "This is how it is and there is no other
> way around it" . . . but if you show students and they get to
> see the problem and actually act it, and then they get to make a
> choice, people feel better or as if they have choices and they feel
> that they made a choice.

Julisa had two difficult roles in the public performances of summer 2008 and 2009. In the summer 2008, after a student artist, Jada (whom you will meet in Act III), left the program abruptly, Julisa was asked to play her character in "Meditations of Our Hearts." "Meditations," written in a Girl Time RYDC workshop, was a story of three friends discussing their past, present, and future lives (Winn, 2010). Set in a detention center, "Meditations" asked enduring questions about how girls found themselves detained in the first place and how they would prepare for life beyond incarceration. Juilsa played, "Aniya," who was hard-headed and unpredictable yet vulnerable. In summer 2009, Julisa played an abusive boyfriend who showed up to his girlfriend's hair salon and threatened her in front of her colleagues and clients. Julisa's performance earned rave reviews from the boys in the RYDC performances. Acting along side the girls was her most important teaching strategy; when she gave her all, the girls gave theirs.

Teaching for Social Justice

Educators working as youth advocates and allies do not have to fit one profile. Members of the Girl Time teaching ensemble represent a variety of views and approaches to their work with girls. Some teaching artists wanted to see youth develop self-discipline and learn how to be accountable for choices, while others questioned, critiqued, and challenged schools, the juvenile justice system, White supremacy, and White privilege. Other teachers fell somewhere in between. All of these teaching artists left themselves open for possibilities; in other words, they did not make up their minds about any girls they encountered in RYDCs or the summer program before a relationship could be cultivated. Teaching artists entered the teaching field through various pathways emerging from living, working, and being active in the lives of and with regard to the issues facing girls and women. Together they became conscientious educators in pursuit of youth justice. In the next act, you will meet the girls who were benefactors of the work, commitment, and dedication of the Girl Time teachers.

"We Try to Find Our Way Home"

Formerly Incarcerated Girls Speak

Date: Monday, June 25, 2007. Location: Main RYDC. Weather: Warm, cacophonous thunder with torrential downpours. "Were there any characters or plays you could relate to?" Zaire asked the audience of boys and girls at Main RYDC. In a rare opportunity, male and female detainees were brought together to engage in discussion of social issues emerging from the plays written and performed by Girl Time ensemble members. After countless emails, phone conversations, and even some outright begging, Kaya convinced the detention center facility to allow our ensemble to perform for incarcerated boys and girls. Initially the facility was concerned that it could be dangerous to bring formerly incarcerated girls back to the facility where they were once housed. After some deliberation, the facility finally decided to allow the performance to take place as long as all of the student artists went through an extensive search. Kaya agreed with one stipulation; teachers would have to endure the same search procedures as the girls side by side. One of the girls in the RYDC audience responded to Zaire, "I like the runaway girl 'cause a lot of us have run away too." "Okay," Zaire continued, "Here are my ground rules. You can talk about your business but don't be talkin' about what others do or did." Nodding her head in affirmation the same girl amended her response, "I like the runaway. I can relate because I have runaway too." Another girl's hand waved wildly until Zaire acknowledged her with, "I see you sis." "I like the play with the girl whose mom found out she was gay because I went through the same thing. You know the play about they dyke?" Zaire immediately offered, "You mean the lesbian? Yes." Too eager to share her story the girl seemingly ignored Zaire's word suggestion. "I like girls too so I understand and parents respond differently." This was one of the first times I saw such a large group of boys seemingly speechless, yet, intensely watching and listening as suggested by the way many of them sat forward in their seats, exchanged glances with each other without speaking, and occasionally smiled. "Did anything in these plays make you think differently?" probed Zaire. A pause ensued until one girl from the audience offered, "Most girls think they can't get out of bad situations but some of the girls in the plays did." Many JCOs and teaching artists smiled at this response, while Zaire nodded and smiled before turning toward the student artists who were seated facing the audience. "Do any of the actors want to say anything?" In an uncharacteristically trembling voice, Nia began, "It's a wonderful thing to be on the outside." Her declaration was met with complete stillness and silence while all eyes were fixed on her. Nia courageously continued, "Start thinking now about what you want to do so when you get home you can do it." As her voice trailed off giving way to nervousness and the reality that the entire room watched, waited, and listened, Sanaa picked up where her friend and fellow ensemble member left off, "Don't let anybody steal your dreams from you." As Sanaa and Nia exchanged supportive smiles, an unexpected voice came from the back of the room. Overwhelmed by the performance and dialogue that ensued, a Black female JCO shouted, "I'm proud of all my girls. I love you but I don't ever want to see you again!"

Talking back may be the most important pedagogical practice that Girl Time enlists. Our Place Theatre Company set itself apart from other theatre companies in the area by underscoring its commitment to community dialogue. Girl Time followed the same principles. After each performance, whether it was part of a Girl Time RYDC workshop, the summer public performance, or student artists returning to the RYDCs to perform, a "talk-back" followed. Talk-backs invited those who witnessed stories in motion written by incarcerated girls to engage formerly incarcerated girls in a discussion about how they experienced the work, the process of preparing for a performance, and their next steps. Talk-back audiences included parents, guardians (foster parents, group home leaders), siblings and other family members, JCOs, probation officers, supporters of the arts, people who read about the project in the newspaper, and people with varying degrees of understanding of the criminal and juvenile justice system. In the opening vignette, Zaire facilitates a talk-back after the Girl Time ensemble performed at Main RYDC in which incarcerated youth were invited to discuss what they appreciated about the plays. Nia, a Girl Time student artist who participated in the summer 2007, 2008, and 2009 programs, and Sanaa who also participated in the summer 2007 and 2009 programs, found another purpose for the talk-back. Talking back, in this context, gave Nia and Sanaa a forum to encourage their peers to think about what was beyond the confines of the detention center facility and to plan boldly for their new possible lives.

The purpose of Act III is to illuminate the fluidity and range of formerly incarcerated girls who cannot be relegated to a single story. Through a synthesis of qualitative interview data with Girl Time summer program participants, you are invited to see formerly incarcerated girls in their full humanity. Nia, Sanaa, Jada, Lisa, and Janelle present their historicized selves—that is, their narratives about how they experienced their young lives in addition to their lives prior to incarceration, during incarceration, and through their transition to physical and psychological freedom are accompanied by observed activity and engagement. These profiles were constructed from formerly incarcerated girls' stories that I mined from interview data focusing on (1) growing up; (2) experiences leading up to incarceration; (3) experiences with the Girl Time program including relationships to themes and plots in the plays, empathy for particular characters, and their relationship to fellow student and teaching artists; and (4) imagining their future lives. Through the girls' narratives, you will see the girls at work in their theatre craft and ensemble building as they prepare for their own performances of possibilities. And, finally, you will hear the girls' voices in concert with one another. All interviews were conducted at the multi-service center where the staff was gracious enough to provide the brightest space in the building (a conference room with cheerful orange walls) and comfortable chairs. Interviews lasted, on average, for 30 minutes in between cast meetings and rehearsals. In some cases I was able to meet the girls before a day's work in the summer program, but when time constraints made that impossible, I had to conduct interviews at the public theater during our last 2 days of rehearsal.

In her examination of "Black girlhood," Brown (2008) argues, "Adults working with girls in creative capacities who do feel compelled to share girls' work have not just a responsibility but an obligation to declare how they themselves were changed by the process" (p. 114). One thing I learned from my work with the Power Writers—a community of youth poets from the Bronx—is that as a Black woman scholar I do not have the luxury to sit back, observe, and take notes without contributing to the community in some way, nor would I want to because there is too much work to be done (Fisher, 2005a, 2005b, 2007; Winn & Ubiles, in press). Brown's declaration raises a critical issue in qualitative research, especially for ethnographers; when and where does the ethnographer's learning unfold and how is that interpreted alongside an analysis of the data? Like many of the teaching artists, I saw glimpses of my teen life in the girls' lives but also saw how privileged I had been to have so many advocates during my teen years. I also realize how naïve I had been as a teacher; certainly, I knew that some of my students were encountering the juvenile justice system. However I would simply welcome students back who "went away" for a time period without knowing how to really support them as they returned to school. Even early in my teaching career I had a sense that referrals were indeed a part of a paper trail for particular students that I did not want to contribute to, and I tried to handle all incidents "in house." I can still see the look on one of my student's faces when I gave him a referral; it was the first and last time I ever wrote one and I felt an overwhelming sense of betrayal, as did my student.

My university teaching was also impacted by my work with the girls; in my graduate courses, such as "Literacy as a Civil Right," I devoted a significant amount of time to school-to-prison-pipeline issues and policy reports. It was often helpful to build a bridge between these issues and the importance of thinking about education and literacy in particular as a civil right (Greene, 2008; Lunsford, Moglen, & Slevin, 1990; Plaut, 2009). Additionally, I integrated readings about the school-to-prison pipeline in my syllabus for my preservice English teachers, because I found that many classroom teachers did not have a clue about how they were intimately involved in the ushering of children from schools to jails. In fact, many teachers, out of inexperience and fear, were simply trying to survive and wanted to get students who were generating discomfort out of their rooms. My work in the local high schools was also influenced by interviewing and analyzing interview transcripts; I integrated readings into faculty forums for high school teachers in all content areas about zero-tolerance policies and surveillance in urban public schools. Perhaps most importantly, I renewed my commitment to the Girl Time teaching artists every year by compiling resource binders for the annual teacher training. With the help of research assistants, I assembled materials ranging from scholarly articles to stories from newspapers and other periodicals that were relevant to the school-to-prison pipeline and, more specifically, the incarceration of girls and women.

It did not take long before I began to realize while doing this work that I needed multiple perspectives to understand the importance of the work. I joined a working group called "Behind the Cycle: An Integrative Approach to Justice Reform" (BTC). In the context of this working group I learned from lawyers, many of whom referred to themselves as "recovering defense attorneys" who started nonprofit organizations focused on youth advocacy; judges; housing authority administrators; psychological health workers; scholars in various fields; and policymakers from "the hill." Together we heard from men and women working with the children of incarcerated parents, considered the ways in which Black and Latino youth have been targeted, and exchanged white papers from various institutions.

Interviewing the girls was not only humbling but transforming for me as an ethnographer, teaching artist, and human being concerned about youth justice. Girls often cited their interview experience as one of their favorite parts of the program, which was an unintended yet welcome consequence. Kaya, Anne, and I soon realized this was a necessary part of the process. The girls interviewed me as well. At the end of every interview they had an opportunity to ask me questions, which included, "Why do you work with us? Do you like working with us? Why? How did you learn about Girl Time? How long did you go to school? Do you have any children? Why not? What do you like about us?" From the personal to the professional, the girls had a right to know as much about us as we knew about them. Interviews also became a way to communicate the needs and concerns students had with the Girl Time teaching artist ensemble so teachers could adjust and make immediate changes to their practice when and where relevant. I was able to share important issues that emerged from interviews with the teaching artists to better inform our practice. Sometimes this happened immediately (during teacher meetings after summer program sessions) or at the aforementioned annual teacher training, which included new and returning teachers.

I also learned that my original interview protocol was not as helpful as I initially believed. Once I was sitting face to face with each girl, it seemed too bureaucratic to have this list of questions, knowing that this particular community experienced sitting across from countless adults with their folders, documents, and paperwork, asking them questions, making notes and judgments. I allowed the interviews with student artists to unfold with guiding questions asking girls about their lives before detainment and what it was like growing up and going to school. Every interview was videotaped, digitized, and transcribed. Prior to the interviews I also asked girls if they wanted to be recorded (either video recorded or audio recorded using iPod technology). I also asked girls if they preferred that I sit with them in the video frame or if they wanted to appear on camera alone. Most of the girls asked me to sit in the frame with them, while others relished in the experience of being the sole subject of the video camera.

It was, of course, optional for girls to discuss what life experiences and events they believed led to their incarceration; however, all of the girls who I interviewed launched into this dialogue without hesitation almost as if they had been waiting for an opportunity to tell their side of the story (Winn, 2010). Many shared with me that throughout their incarceration process they were never invited to share their perspectives, especially in juvenile court. After years of interviewing youth in my research and activism, I felt an overwhelming responsibility to encourage young people to use a critical lens and interrogate their experiences as well. After the summer 2007 cohort interviews I realized I was getting a standard narrative, which I refer to as incarceration discourse. For example student artists in my study framed their lives in three phases, including, (1) I was born; (2) I mysteriously turned bad (this was always around the middle school years); (3) I deserved my punishment and now I am going to "be good" or "do good" again." Elsewhere scholars have found evidence of incarceration discourse in their work with formerly incarcerated men and women. Meiners describes this formulaic writing as the "redemptive genre" (Meiners, 2007, p. 140) and saw much of it in the autobiographic writing at the high school where she works with formerly incarcerated men and women.

My interview questions had to change to move beyond this so-called incarceration discourse, which embodies the pathologization Meiners critiques. The problem with embracing the "I turned bad" narrative is that many incarcerated and formerly incarcerated youth have not developed the critical literacies that would enable them to "seriously challenge the institutional narratives and media images that represent them as violent and uneducable and that contribute to the notion that imprisonment is a reasonable, if not natural, option in their lives" (Duncan, 2000, p. 39). During the interviews, I noted how often girls referenced the need to "do good" and "do better" without any real knowledge of how to begin that process or even a strong definition of what it meant to "do good" or "do better." I began to ask girls what would have to change in the world around them so that they could live the lives they desired. I am not the only scholar to understand that this question must be included in an interview protocol for incarcerated and formerly incarcerated girls and women. In their interrogation of "gendered justice" or working with incarcerated women, Covington and Bloom (2003) enlist a similar question, "How could things in your community have been different to help prevent you from being here?"

Throughout this chapter you will hear the voices of Nia, Sanaa, Jada, Lisa, and Janelle. While I interviewed 21 girls throughout the tenure of the study, in this act I focus on girls who participated in the Girl Time summer program in at least two of the three summers between 2006 and 2009 when this study took place. Wisdom from Nia, Sanaa, Jada, Lisa, and Janelle will extend beyond this act and will echo throughout acts IV and V along with the voices of their peers. The ability to interview girls for more than one summer provided insight into their growth and development. Multiple interviews demonstrated the complexities of the girls' lives and dismantled the notion of a single story of incarcerated and formerly incarcerated youth.

"I Came Back to Deliver a Message": Nia

"I like playing basketball. I like meeting new people. It's a fun experience. I love going shopping, talking on the phone sometimes, it all depends on who it is. I like learning new things," Nia excitedly shared when asked to introduce herself. I met Nia right after she turned 16 during the summer 2007 program. Nia always had a job and loved making her own money: "I'm working now and before Girl Time I was playing basketball and going to basketball camps. I'd go to [basketball camps] and sometimes we'll just gather up a team and play basketball for fun. Sometimes I be with my sister and my cousins just mellow, chillin', coolin'." Nia often punctuated her sentences by smiling widely at the video camera that she chose to face alone. Like the stage, the video camera inspired a liveliness in Nia who was otherwise reserved and intent with observing others closely. Born in the city and proudly boasting she was a "Jackson Hills baby"—the public hospital overwhelmingly known as the hospital one goes to when he or she gets shot or stabbed—Nia attended public schools. Nia was supposed to enter 11th grade in the fall. While I asked Nia to talk about herself she quickly launched into a series of events leading to her incarceration. Nia, who identified herself as a "female stud," asserted that her school experiences were inextricably linked to her sexual identity.

In the previous school year, while Nia was still 15, she was confronted by a female romantic interest's brother. According to Nia, she and the girl established their mutual attraction and interest in each other, which infuriated the girl's brother. "He ended up finding out [his sister] was gay or what not. He thought I had did it to her but . . . she was like this before I even met her." Nia did not fit into the heteronormative expectations of girls—especially in the southeastern Bible belt. Nia wore her hair in a series of small plaits strewn all over her head. Her jeans, always baggy and sagging, were adorned with an array of designs and sparkling materials on her pockets. Nia walked with great confidence and with what the youth proudly refer to as swagger, which was typically designated for boys. Nia informed the other girls in the Girl Time program that she was gay, and everyone adored Nia as demonstrated by friendly hugs, conversation, and even playful teasing. While Nia's recounting of this confrontation with her romantic interest's brother could have been a case of homophobic bullying, the school's response could also have been cloaked in homophobia. Once the school security team (all male) intervened, they accepted Nia's attacker's story and proceeded to search Nia. They found a pocketknife.

Nia's pocketknife was not involved in the confrontation and she claimed she was so accustomed to carrying it with her that she forgot she had it at school. Nevertheless, this pocketknife would have serious ramifications for Nia. Without naming the homophobic actions of her assailant and unable to question why male security guards were allowed to search her, Nia went on to say she served 3 months at Main RYDC. Richie (2005) argues that lesbian youth are often subjected to discrimination in the juvenile justice system. Interviews with lesbian youth revealed that many carried weapons in order to protect themselves from homophobic predators. There were also girls who exchanged services such as drug dealing and prostitution for protection from male counterparts who were feared in their communities.

Recognizing Nia's light, one of the Department of Juvenile Justice (DJJ) administrators and Nia's probation officer immediately thought of Nia when they heard about the Girl Time summer program. Nia's probation officer thought she would make a talented actor and Nia liked the thought of helping other girls through her performance. During summer 2007, Nia played a range of characters, but there was one character in particular that Nia was excited about. In "The Ruby Show" Nia played "Li'l Rico" who was "a female stud lady" coming out to her mother on a televised talk show:

> "The Ruby Show" I can relate to. When I was—I think I was 14, I was staying at this group home and I met this girl and we started talking, talking, and talking. We ended up "kicking it" and liking each other. So, the group home found out and they ended up calling my mother. My mother called me and she asked me, "So, what's this I'm hearing about you supposed to be gay?" I was like, "Well, what are you talking about?" At first that's what I said because I know how my mama is. I just thought she was going to flip out but we had a talk and then she was like, "Why did I have to find out the hard way?" I was like, "I didn't know how you was going to react to it." She was like, "Well it was not something I approve of but you my daughter and I gotta get used to this." (Interview, June 2007)

Playing Li'l Rico also provided Nia with a way to introduce herself to the Girl Time ensemble. Li'l Rico affirmed Nia and Nia affirmed Li'l Rico; featuring this character and this play in the summer 2007 program demonstrated to the girls that sexual identity and the process of "coming out" were important, timely, and relevant topics that Girl Time approached with respect.

Nia loved to perform; however, she was very skeptical about returning to Main to perform for other incarcerated youth, " I said I wasn't going back period! I don't want to step foot [inside], I don't want to visit nobody. I mean they can call me, but I really don't want to go back. When I heard [my performance] is helping them or trying to help them I was like, "Okay I guess I can try to do this," but I was really nervous when they said I was going back to Main!" In my analysis of interview data, girls universally expressed a reluctance returning to Main or any other RYDC to perform; however, every girl did it in spite of their initial apprehension. "Walking through the front door" of Main, as opposed to being corralled through the back (which was the prisoner entry), was a consistently triumphant moment throughout the transcripts. Nia was compelled by the possibility that she could help her peers through her performance, "I can tell others some of the decisions that they should make, some of the decisions they should not make . . . Sometimes I feel that we—as in me and my peers— can try to relay a message to [incarcerated girls] . . . they will probably listen a little bit because we around the same age and we experienced the same thing . . . I'm sure they want to get older, be something, and do something with themselves. So, I try to motivate." In Nia's performance of possibilities, she not only wanted to have a positive impact on her peers but also the Main RYDC staff:

> [My participation] lets them know that I'm out doing the right thing. That I'm not making bad decisions that I'm not supposed to do. It also lets them know that they won't be seeing me no more except for [my performance]. Well most of them was telling me, "I'm not going to see you back in here am I?" I was like, "No, you really won't unless I'm working here or something." (Interview, June 2007)

Soon after Isis and I took the Girl Time ensemble to see a production of "The Bluest Eye" in the fall of 2007, Nia's phone was disconnected. All of us were worried yet hopeful she would show up some time. Like teachers everywhere we chased current phone numbers and found ourselves deeply disappointed when our students' numbers were out of service. On the first day of the summer 2008 program, Nia strolled in late but with a look that announced, "I'm here!" Teachers and fellow students screamed. We exchanged hugs and returned to our circle, knowing we would catch up later. At this point Nia had more job experience; she left a fast food restaurant for a grocery store and worked whenever she was not in school. She considered herself more mature because she learned how to "run away" from the crowds as opposed to "running towards" them:

> Like, say a crowd fighting or something like that; I don't run over to it like I used to. Instead, I be like, "Oh man, what they fighting for? It ain't called for." And I just go on my way. Or if I'm at work and my manager make me mad or something, I just work on polite and say, "Yes sir, yes ma'am." I just do my work. And that's it. (Interview, June 2008)

What struck me about Nia was her sense that she did not have complete control or power over whether or not she would be incarcerated again. In Nia's mind, her encounters with the juvenile justice system caught her by surprise and she believed in the power of getting "jinxed" more than anything:

It was kind of interesting to be back inside of [Main RYDC] to perform without actually being inside of there. So when I saw the JCOs, I knew I would be doing something good. So I would just smile and I kind of got to see a silly side of them. But I tried to keep it professional at that time. So it was a good experience. I was kind of shaking at first because I thought it might jinx me to go back to jail or something like that. When I left the facility, I [didn't] wanna go back. It kind of made me a little shaky, I thought I was back there . . . Because you know, after you leave, you not supposed to take nothing back with you. Like numbers and stuff like that. Personally, I don't try to keep in touch with people that been there with me, because you know, they might be a bad influence on me. They might make me do something that I don't normally do. So I might try to stay away from them if I know my limits. But jinxing? I feel like if I go back there, I might just end up back in there or something. So I try not to go back unless I'm going there for something good. But I was kind of nervous because I know I had not been there before, and then they were gonna be watching me, like "She's been doing good I guess" and then some folks, they judge you wrong. (Interview, June 2008)

Nia confirmed the teaching artists' worst fear; she returned to Main earlier that year, which was why we were unable to reach her. Again, Nia's trouble began at school and involved the school security team. According to Nia, she found "a fancy little lighter" and put it in the pocket of the pants that she usually reserved for work. Rushing to school one morning she wore her black work pants without thinking twice about the new treasure she pocketed earlier that week. Nia was in the hallway after the bell rang with a pass and "an officer" stopped to question why she was in the hallway. Even though she had a pass, Nia claimed the officer started to search her. What I found troubling throughout my conversation with Nia is that she did not know if this was a school security guard or an actual police officer. She had never seen this man in the school before and did not know his name. During the search, he found her lighter. Nia said she did not realize that this lighter also had a blade; however the security guard or police officer continued to tinker with it and found that it did. At that point she was restrained, searched, handcuffed, and pepper sprayed when she tried to use her cell phone to call her mother. At some point a second officer—also a male—got involved:

So by the time I put the phone back in my pocket, both of them slammed me on the ground and threw me in the handcuffs. So after that, I looked to the left to see if anyone was in the hallway to see what was going on. So he just pulled out the pepper spray and sprayed me. And he's talking about how he shouldn't have had to slam me on the ground. He took me into the restroom and was putting water on my face. And I was telling him I couldn't breathe. So I asked him to stop putting water on my face. So my mom finally came, and they sent me to jail. They were trying to give me 18 months. (Interview, June 2008)

By the time Ms. Johnson, Nia's mother, arrived, the school had already made the decision to involve the police. Nia was facing a charge of "carrying a concealed weapon at school." Nia and Ms. Johnson never met with a principal or administrator of any sort. Nia's teachers, who felt powerless during the incident, wrote letters on her behalf:

Nia: I know my teachers, and there were a lot of teachers from different schools who sent letters telling the judge how good I had been, how I had done found jobs, I was working. I had stayed out of trouble for a whole year and a half, so why would I just up and want to get into some trouble now? So I guess [the judge] saw it was no intention to do nothing wrong. And she gave me 60 days. And the man, he was trying to give me 18 months.
Maisha: Who was this man?
Nia: I don't know, I know that he was against me. He wasn't with me. Whoever that man is. He was like, he was a Caucasian, and he was like, "She needs to be in jail. You need to give her 2 years instead of 18 months."
Maisha: This is someone in the school or the court?
Nia: The courtroom.
Maisha: The attorney?
Nia: Yea.
Maisha: Do you think it was the prosecuting attorney?
Nia: Yea. [The prosecutor] was like, "Look at her past records." But that didn't matter because everyone was saying I had changed. But he was like, "Look at her past records, there's nothing new" and all this. Just trying to make me just sound bad. So I'm just sitting over there praying. Praying and praying. And then my mom was trying to ask if I could get

time served, because I was already in Main for like 2 months without me getting my time. But [the judge] said she wasn't gonna give me time served. I was like, "OK, that's fine with me. Sixty days against eighteen months. That's alright." So they shipped me off April 29, 2008, to an RYDC in [another city]. (Interview, June 2008)

Being sentenced to an RYDC in another city was a hardship for Nia's family, who was already transportation challenged. Therefore, Nia was unable to receive the visits and support that she needed during that time. However, Nia was so happy to have 60 days as opposed to 18 months that she did not dwell on location. Nia was unable to name the people who were a part of the decisionmaking at school and in the courtroom; she just knew "they was against me—they wasn't for me" without knowing their names, roles, or titles. I wanted to know more about how these two incidents that took place at school impacted her and if she could see a relationship between the two·

Well, that situation, it's like, I didn't even see that coming. Just like the last situation that just happened. I didn't see that coming. You know, I'm thinking I'm just going to go to school. And then get out and go straight to work, but when I was being searched, you know, I didn't know there was [a] blade on there, so I'm thinking he might just put me in [in-school suspension, or ISS] or something like that, but now, I don't know, I just say everything happens for a reason. I'm glad I didn't get that 18 months because that would have been a big setback, because the schools in jail, they aren't set right. (Interview, June 2008)

We had a lengthy conversation about school in the detention centers; Nia believed detention center schools could not prepare students for graduation and had limited course offerings for 11th and 12th graders. Nia was adamant that she needed to find another job to "keep me out of a lot of trouble" and surround herself with positive people:

Maisha: When you talk about keeping out of a lot of trouble, what are the things that would have to change around you. Not you, but around you, for that trouble to not exist. If you could have the ideal world or situation, what would you need so that those things weren't even a factor?
Nia: Positive people.

Maisha: Positive people?

Nia: Because some folks, they try to down me. Some people say because of my sexuality that I might not be nothing, and, you know, 'cause of the charges that I have, they might look at that and might not accept that at a job, but I don't believe it. I don't believe it. I really don't. So I feel like I gotta make a story out of them.

Maisha: Make a story out of them?

Nia: Make a story out of them, you know. I don't want that to be true. I don't want to make them seem like, "I told you so." So all I look forward to is making me, my momma, the positive people that be around me that help me, and my sister proud.

Maisha: Are there any other things around you that would have to change so that you could walk the path that you want to walk?

Nia: Long as the positive people are around me, I think I got the rest. There's a lot of stuff I could take. I'm not gonna give up. That ain't me. Long as those folks around me keep me up, help me out when I need it, I got the rest. (Interview, June 2008)

Nia's return to Girl Time was her effort to surround herself with "positive people" who would support, uplift, and certainly accept her. On one hand, Nia saw her troubles with the law and potential for getting into trouble as being random or a result of being jinxed; however, she did not give herself credit for going to the well from which she drank deeply to provide her with the confidence she needed to get through another year. Making every effort to participate in the Girl Time summer program was Nia's way of seizing control; in the program there were rituals, yet, an openness to new experiences. Girl Time offered a positive peer network for Nia and a relationship with teachers who had a wealth of life experiences and wisdom to share.

Nia and I consistently stayed in touch during the next year, and Nia returned for the summer 2009 program. At this point she was working in a fast food pizza place and lived with her sister, whom she adored, her brother-in-law, and her nephew. Nia's family was experiencing extreme financial hardships and she carried pizza home daily to help defray meal costs. "Now when I eat pizza, I throw up," Nia explained. Nia's financial hardships forced her to work many hours, and when other family members lost their jobs she made up for it by working even harder. Nia felt that she and her mother needed space from each other. However, Nia's main worry during the summer 2009 program was whether or not her mother would attend the final performance. All of the teaching artists took turns calling Nia's mother and inviting her, underscoring how much Nia wanted her to be there—she showed up! Nia, who was always supporting the other girls, needed our support this particular summer. She decided that once she graduated (she was still trying to get through the graduation exam for social studies) she would join the military. Initially I thought Nia did not trust herself to make good decisions; however, I began to realize that Nia did not trust her surroundings. Nia never felt entirely safe, and she wanted to be somewhere (other than jail) that had structure and where she could stay "out of trouble":

> It's like I put myself in situations where like either you can do this, or you can do that. And I [went] in the facility at the time where I [had] to make a quick decision, well at least back then I was in the facility. So it was peer pressure, sometimes it really wasn't my fault at times. But now, I feel like I'm doing good. I grew up, I feel like I'm more mature than I was when I was, you know, doing stuff I have no business doing. And, yea, I'm doing good. (Interview, June 2009)

Girls who have become victims of the school-to-prison pipeline have more responsibilities and worries outside of school (Simkins et al., 2004). There was nothing Nia wanted more than to focus on her studies and graduate. Nia also yearned for order and structure, thus, making military an attractive option to her. The Girl Time program supported Nia as she began the process of learning how to trust herself, believe in her own instincts, and make positive decisions for her future.

"Where I Can Feel Free All the Time": Sanaa

"Right now I'm in 10th grade. I am trying to pursue the career of being a criminal lawyer. I like doing hair and stuff. I like to dance, sing, write, and read." Sanaa was a walking advertisement for her ability to "do hair"; she frequently wore a coif of long and extraordinarily compact braids with a streak of unexpected color (red was her favorite). Sometimes she pulled them back into a loose ponytail or let them fall past her shoulders. Whenever she received compliments she proudly responded, "Thank you. I did it myself." Sanaa had eight brothers and sisters ("You know, it's kind of hectic at times") whom she adored ("I love my brothers and sisters. I love children period!"). As she introduced herself, Sanaa grazed the concept of freedom—a concept she admittedly was getting accustomed to with time:

> Just basically in my spare time I don't do things that the other kids do like go out and party all the time. And get themselves in trouble. I have been locked up a couple of times. And you know it's kind of hard but I am doing my best to stay out of trouble. It is going well for me, you know. I am used to it, well, I am not really used to it, but I am tired of being somewhere where I can't do what I want to do—I am not free to do what I want to do. So I want to make a change and become someone who makes certain decisions for herself. (Interview, June 2007)

Sanaa's inclusion of her incarceration experiences in her personal introduction during the interview could have been a strategy to demonstrate her before and after self. Distinguishing herself from her peers who "party all the time" and "get themselves in trouble," Sanaa presented herself not only as someone desiring freedom but also deserving freedom. Initially Sanaa declared she is "used to" staying "out of trouble," however, she amended this statement with, "Well, I'm not really used to it, but I'm tired of being somewhere I can't do what I want to do. [Where] I am not free to do what I want to do." For Sanaa freedom and the ability to make decisions for herself were synonymous.

It was difficult for Sanaa to disentangle her experiences growing up and her life in detention. I met Sanaa in Main RYDC when she was 15; however, she "started going to Meadow RYDC" first, which was outside of the city. At Meadow, "the bread was soft and the JCOs were like mothers," explained Sanaa who first went there at the age 13. However, after countless returns (she thinks maybe eight but was not sure) she was sent to Main when Meadow was full. Main's facility contrasted sharply with Meadow ("[At Main] the clothes and sheets had stains on them and it was not clean . . . "). When it seemed that I would have to raise the question of how this cycle started, I did so tentatively:

> *Maisha*: Do you feel up to talking about the things that led to your going to Meadow and Main?
> *Sanaa*: Um hmm.
> *Maisha*: You could talk about it or you can pass. It's your choice.
> *Sanaa*: I can talk about it. Well, really, how it started is like you

know I was getting in trouble a lot in school. I wanted to
be this big bully person or whatever. It got me in trouble
a lot and then at home. You know at first my mom didn't
have a lot of discipline with us. She just talked to us or
whatever. But then when she started [disciplining us] it
made me mad so I would go outside and be with friends
and boyfriends and whatever and do whatever they did. I
was hanging around the wrong crowd. The first thing I got
locked up for was driving a stolen car. Actually, it was my
boyfriend who stole the car and you know I took the blame
for it or whatever. You know trying to feel like I was doing
something at the time but really I was being stupid. And
then I got on probation. You know probation has a lot of
rules like no suspension, go to school every day, and I wasn't
following the rules so I got locked up again, and again, and
again. And then one time when I decided, "You know I am
going to change," it didn't really come from deep down
inside me. It came from what I knew my mother wanted to
hear. (Interview, June 2007)

Citing her desire to be "this big bully person or whatever" at school,
Sanaa saw a relationship between her mother being flexible with rules
("She just talked to us.") to taking disciplinary action. Sanaa's response—
not unlike many youth after struggling with parents—was "hanging
around the wrong crowd" to "do whatever they did." When Sanaa "stole"
a car (or took the blame for her boyfriend stealing a car), she did not realize she was entering a long-term relationship with the juvenile justice
system. Sanaa initially did not understand that the experience with DJJ
would also impact school and vice versa ("you know probation has a lot of
rules like no suspension, go to school every day . . . "). After being "locked
up again and again and again," Sanaa adopted elements of incarceration
discourse. Later, I learned that Sanaa and her siblings had been divided up
among separate foster homes. They ran away from those foster homes to
the same location to reunite and as a result were arrested. This short-lived
reunion ended with more time in the detention center for Sanaa. However,
what I find compelling and incredibly honest was Sanaa's reflection about
her declaration of change ("It really didn't come from deep down inside
me. It came from what I knew my mother wanted to hear."). Sanaa's wisdom and frankness were refreshing. She had the ability to name things
in a way that were beyond her years. And while I was taken back by her

account of attempting to steal another car by throwing a rock at the car window in order to stop the driver, I was also surprised by Sanaa's ability to tell the story. The woman in the car stopped, backed up, and through a sea of tears asked Sanaa and her friend why they would do such a thing. I wondered what I would have done had I been the woman in the car. I was equally curious about why Sanaa and her friend stayed with the woman, knowing they were in trouble, until the police arrived rather than running away from the incident; however, Sanaa simply did not know why she stayed.

I learned from Sanaa that when we met at a Girl Time workshop in Main in 2006, she was serving her time for the attempted car robbery incident. Since she had "been locked up a lot of times," she served "4 or 5 months" at Main for this offense. It was the longest time she ever spent in a detention center. Sanaa made an impression on all of the teaching artists during the workshop at Main; she gave everything her full effort, from physical warm-ups to the games to the playwriting process:

> Well at first [pass the clap] was kind of weird. It is kind of hard
> at first and you don't want everyone laughing at you. But, you
> know Girl Time actually make you feel like family really. If you
> mess up and people laugh, people are laughing with you not
> at you. So, it is kind of funny you know. I would have never
> thought of anything like that. You know, putting your feelings
> into a big ball and put your good feelings in too—you know stuff
> like that. (Interview, June 2007)

Sanaa peered at all of us over the top of her smart-looking glasses during the first day of the workshop. She seldom smiled during our first encounter and she looked rather skeptical about everything. Sanaa reminded me of a savvy businesswoman; she did everything with dedication and precision, and she encouraged her peers to be team players. Sanaa shared her impressions of the teaching artists and the Girl Time program:

> Well, I didn't really know that it was coming or whatever. I
> didn't know what it was about. The [JCOs] just picked certain
> people that was doing good and sat us in the room with ya'll or
> whatever. It was kind of interesting you know because usually
> in jail you don't feel like you are free. So when we was able to
> write plays, tell what we wanted, how the plays was going to
> go, what the play would be about, it made me feel free and it

made me want to be out in the open world and not be locked up . . . Well, we split up in sections or whatever and you told us to pick out the name for the play. I'm used to writing. I like to write a lot. I felt like I was at a place that I was comfortable at the time, and then when ya'll left I realized that it was feeling free at the time. I was thinking, well, you know, I want to be out where I can feel free all the time, not just one time in my life. (Interview, June 2007)

Sanaa's play, "Ride or Die," was wildly popular with her peers, the teaching artists, and the audience who first saw it in Main (see Appendix C for the entire "Ride or Die" script). Coauthored with a peer, "Ride or Die" encapsulated many incarcerated girls' experiences and the play examined a central concept that emerged from many of the other plays. "Ride or Die" was an example of Freire's challenge that teachers must become knowledgeable in the language of their students. Sanaa offered a multi-dimensional definition of this concept as well as examples:

"Ride or Die" [usually refers to] a man and his woman, and the woman is like his sidekick. Whatever he does, she does—that's the "ride" part. The "die" part is if you are not going to do it, then you are going to take the consequences that I am going to give you. That's what most of these girls get in trouble for, their boyfriends. They really not realizing that they are taking the blame for whatever their boyfriend is doing. Some of them do realize eventually when they get this long period of [jail] time or whatever. (Interview, June 2007)

Sanaa not only defined ride or die but could actually critique it as a practice. Every RYDC workshop produced a play that involved this concept. Indeed the ride or die trope is prevalent in urban America where some young women have become "drug mules," withheld evidence from law enforcement in order to cover their boyfriends or partners, and have been convinced that as a woman or a girl they will not get into as much trouble as their male counterparts. Stories like "Kemba's Nightmare," discussed in the Prologue, depicted the reality that young women and girls were "casualties in the drug war" just as much as young men (Smith, 2005, p. 107). On the outset one could easily point a finger towards hip hop music and culture as people often do when there are problems concerning youth culture. Tupac's famed song "Me and My Girlfriend" certainly had its share of radio play as did Jay-Z and Beyonce's remake of the song. In these songs, girls or women follow the male's lead for better or for worse. Women who are "down to" ride or die are upheld as devoted, dependable, and worthy of a man's attention and commitment. Consequently, those who are not down to ride or die are viewed as cowardly, untrustworthy, and replaceable, if not disposable. Both songs specifically cite the notorious crime couple Bonnie and Clyde. The fact that this young White criminal couple in Texas in the 1930s has somehow influenced the lives of incarcerated teen girls and urban youth throughout the United States is not completely unexplainable, given that the ethos of Bonnie and Clyde hovers over American popular culture. While the most obvious artifact may be Warren Beatty and Faye Dunaway's version of *Bonnie and Clyde*, released in 1967, American popular culture has always enjoyed its share of gangster movies and entertainment with a clear "rebel/criminal." Fraden (2001) argues:

> The rebel/criminal has always been an object of fascination in modern times . . . but alongside fascination, and even glorification, is a heightened fear of the criminal and political manipulation of that fear. (p. 128)

For teen girls like Sanaa who are facing abject poverty, the rebel/criminal fascination can have severe repercussions beyond movies, songs, and video games. Young people, and teen girls in particular, read and critique these images especially in a climate where they are becoming—to borrow Meiners' (2007) term—*public enemies*. However, it is not enough to consider the ways popular culture influences girls to participate in these relationships. Readings or misreadings of popular culture can also impact public policy and peoples' perceptions of who gets counted as a criminal and who is considered a citizen. Therefore popular culture, not only shapes the paths that youth select, but also influences how young people are situated in public policy.

In many ways the pedagogy of playwriting and performance provided a forum for Sanaa to critique the ride or die concept and the negative impact it had on her and her peers. Sanaa's "Ride or Die" told the story of a tangled web involving a "hustler" named Smoke, his loving and naïve wife, Ashley, and his "ride or die chick," named Star. Sanaa described her play with fervor as if she had just left a movie theatre:

> ["Ride or Die"] is about a hustler named Smoke and he has a
> wife [Ashley] or whatever. At first they were like real close and

then he got tired of her. So then he got [Star] who would do
everything for him, do what he wanted to do, make his money,
go put his girls on the street or whatever. . . . Smoke started fall-
ing in love with the Star. . . . Smoke decided that you know he
didn't want the wife in his life anymore. [Smoke] decided that
he was going to kill [Ashley] and move on to Star the other girl.
After [Smoke] told Star that he killed his wife or whatever, Star
felt guilty or whatever because she had lied and she just wanted
to just give it all up—being a hustler's girl because she didn't
want to be in the mess that she was in. So, [Star] finally decided
to turn her [Smoke] into the police and [Smoke] was kind of
confused because he thought they was going to be together—he
was gonna "ride" with her forever. But the message was you can
have all your fun at the time or whatever. But soon you realize
that everything you are doing is not good. So soon you will want
to give it all up. So she was like, "I'm not down for this stuff anymore. You can just move on." (Interview, June 2007)

At the end of the play, Star makes a bold declaration when Smoke
(kneeling in handcuffs at the feet of a police officer) pleads, "I thought
you were my ride or die chick!" Star faces the audience with one hand on
her hip and proclaims, "I was down for the ride but I ain't down for the
die!" During the Girl Time Main workshop girls responded to the play
by jumping out of their seats and giving each other high fives. Otherwise
stern JCOs had to succumb to smiles and affirming nods. Teaching artists
acknowledged this declaration as a breakthrough. Zaire, who led this talk-
back, expressed, "I think this is the first time the woman would not allow
herself to be the sacrificial lamb!" Sanaa explained that she and her coauthor decided to show that even in the context of a decision that seemed
to be getting worse with time that one still had choices. For Sanaa, "Ride
or Die" was more than a play—it was a way to confront some of her decisions and prepare for her performance of possibilities as well:

When I first got locked up it was some boyfriends that I was
taking the blame for whatever they was doing. I was trying to be
this person to act like I am not a scared person. I am not going to
snitch on nobody. I knew the people I was hanging out with. If
you would have told on them—they was crazy and they would
do whatever they got to do to get the problem away from them.
So, it's like I was their ride or die girl, but now just like Star when

I finally realized that what I was doing was not making any sense. There was no purpose to what I was doing. I was just getting myself in more and more trouble. I had to stop or I knew that I was gonna be going somewhere I didn't want to be at. I was either going to be just like the wife. He would get tired of me and go to somebody else and he would probably kill me or whatever. So, I didn't want to put myself in that situation. (Interview, June 2007)

Sanaa viewed Star as an everywoman in a sense. According to Sanaa, many girls begin thinking they are having fun but realize the ride must come to an end. Sanaa saw some of her life in Star's character and also underscored the possibility that she could have been Ashley. While the "wife" and "ride or die chick" were positioned as enemies, they were really on the same trajectory (Winn, 2011). Even teaching artists were impacted by this play. Zaire considered the play to be a breakthrough:

Star said she was "down for the ride, but not for the die!!!" I was proud of that shit right there!!! [This] NEVER happens because [girls are] too afraid to look like a sellout . . . And the reason that I love that play is because Star did not play that super classic, superhero shit, thinking "I got to go down with the ship." This ain't my boat, I ain't selling it, and I sure as hell ain't going down with it. The only thing you're gonna be responsible for is your decision in a situation, that's it. And most of the girls [in RYDCs] are there because they were rolling with their little boyfriends. Sanaa's play showed that no matter what the circumstances were, Star was smart enough to be like, "You know what? This ain't my battle and I ain't fighting it!" A lot of our young girls, women period, need to figure out what our battles are and what they aren't. Because a lot of times we fight battles that ain't got nothing to do with us. (Interview, 2007)

Zaire's work with detention centers and prisons inspired many of the workshops she facilitated, encouraging girls and women to learn how to put themselves first. For Zaire, Sanaa's play was refreshing and dismantled the single story of girls and women being enslaved by their partners. Carrie Mae had a similar reaction to the play:

I think the plays that naturally seem to make an honest statement and are not a contrived or "everything happens well and turns out well thing" but does make a statement such as the "Ride or Die" play that make girls think about the choices they are making or will make or have made. Those things that are honest like the girls coming out to their parents have more of an impact on me personally than when we get shows that have themes. (Interview, 2007)

Carrie Mae referenced the pattern she saw in the playwriting; girls wanted to create happy endings, and who could blame them? However, once in a while there were plays that challenged a "happily ever after" ending. Isis was concerned that if Girl Time opened the door to issues such as ride or die then the program would need more resources to support girls in decisionmaking:

I mean even feeding off of what the young sisters bring us like if topics that come up such as the ride or die topic on the first day, [we need to make] sure that we either address it or have a conversation about it or bring their voice into it beyond just what is written on that paper. [We] need to find ways to address it because I don't know if the girls in the prison if they do have opportunities to have that type of discussion around what it all means. (Interview, 2007)

Curious about Sanaa's comparison of the Girl Time Main workshop to feeling free and yearning for this freedom all the time, I asked Sanaa about what it meant to have an opportunity to write this particular play while detained. Freedom was twofold—there was physical freedom but also freedom from the labels, binaries, and judgment. Sanaa viewed this process of playwriting as a way to demonstrate the talents and abilities she and her peers possessed that people would not expect from incarcerated youth:

Well, a lot of people think that just because you're locked up you can't do this and you can't do that. You not going to be this and you not going to be that. But, most stories are from people who have been in situations where they was locked up. It's not a good world for the people who are locked up. Most people who are locked up have more potential, more talent than most of the people out in the open world and [playwriting and performing] made me feel like you know, "OK, I'm [going] to show these people that I'm not just this person who don't have no life. Who ain't gonna be nobody." You know I just want some people to see, don't judge people by what they do. I mean don't judge people by how they doing right now because you never know what their future is going to be like. So, a lot of people can be mean and bad and get locked up, and a lot of people gonna change.

One of the themes I found when analyzing interview data was how Girl Time student artists like Sanaa viewed their participation as an opportunity to show others—namely the naysayers, which could include family, probation officers, a weary public—that they should not be defined by their incarceration. Sanaa's audience was her grandmother who took her into custody after her last release. "I live with my Grandma now, but when I was living with her back then I kind of had a feeling that she was thinking that when I was getting into trouble I wasn't going to be nothing . . . you know like I'm just going to be like my mother [and] my father." For Sanaa, being a playwright and a writer in general brought humanity and dignity into her character. Writing was associated with stability and being productive, studious, and serious. "When I write," Sanaa explained, "[My grandma] comes in my room and be like, 'Oh, she is doing something positive.'"

Displaying this level of productivity aided in reestablishing trust between Sanaa and her grandmother. Being a playwright and an actor was a tool for Sanaa to demonstrate to others what she already knew about herself; she was more than her time served and was capable of creating something that could potentially inspire and transform others. Sanaa was learning to use both spoken and written language in very powerful ways, and this was even more evident when she returned to participate in the summer 2009 program. We missed Sanaa terribly during the summer 2008 but shared her excitement that she and her siblings were reunited with her mother who lived outside the city limits, making transportation to the program difficult. Sanaa believed that continuing her theatre work would help her inspire other girls and her siblings as well:

> I think I was led to be an inspiration to girls of the same age or younger or even older. But I think [playwriting and performing] are a great experience because I think it shows girls that just because you've been locked up, you can do something with your life. We were all in detention centers. I think it's very eye-opening for [incarcerated] girls to see that they aren't bad peo-

ple. I read the article yesterday about Girl Time and [Anne] said in the article that people look at these girls and think they've been in horrible situations, and they're right. But these girls are also very loving. But I think people don't get to see that. For people to see that people their age and people that have been in their situation . . . that we're loving and that we're able to express ourselves in positive ways . . . gives them hope. And I think that inspires girls when they get out. I think most of us, well, people I know . . . have stayed out of jail. (Interview, June 2009)

Sanaa further explained that writing made her feel "very, very powerful" and that she used it as a tool to conquer anger. Her siblings and grandmother saw how writing provided an outlet and it gave Sanaa something to take great pride in as she prepared for her senior year in high school. Performing writing was the way that Sanaa asserted herself as literate and capable of creating something original that impacted the lives of others. Her play "Ride or Die" not only inspired her peers but teachers and parents as well.

"Kinda Proving Myself": Jada

"I like to write poems and dance. That's about it . . . poems about my life and poems about stuff that has happened to me, or nice poems and sometimes funny. Stuff like that . . . I like to write music too. I used to play the violin at school and was just great at that. Then I lost my violin." Born and raised in the urban southeast, Jada's father hailed from Missouri and her mother grew up in a small town outside the major city where Jada was raised. "I am the baby in the family other than my baby because he's the baby," Jada explained. She was 16 years old the first time we sat down together in the summer of 2007 and she boasted that she had "plenty of brothers" (six total) and a "sister I've never met. It's kinda hard because I wish I could see her. They say she looks just like me." Jada also had two stepsisters.

When I met Jada she was focused on raising her 9-month-old son and school had been put on hold, "I'm supposed to be starting back." Jada enthusiastically participated in the Girl Time summer 2006 program and the teaching artists were thrilled to have her return. "I love to act," explained Jada, "That's one of my talents. Everybody got they own talent and I figure acting is one of my talents. It's fun to me because I can act out real life stories that happen to other people, put it in another way—in a fun way or a serious way—so you can understand [that] these stories actually happened." While Jada was at Main RYDC she never participated in one of the Girl Time workshops and when her probation officer told her about the program she thought it was a joke: "My PO was like, 'We do acting classes up here.' I'm like, 'This is a PO center—what kind of acting classes do you do?'" Jada and her mother studied the Girl Time literature and decided it would be a great way for Jada to pursue her passion and be productive. "I like to perform in front of people because it just lets them know that I can be better than a lot of this other stuff that I have done. I'm kinda proving myself but at the same time I am doing something I like to do. They see me at Main RYDC and see me [as having done] bad things. But me performing and showing them my talents and what I'm able to do—I like doing that. They looking at me like she really doing something with herself instead of running around the streets or getting locked up or fighting. She's participating in something and trying."

Like Sanaa, Jada's performance of possibilities was as much about "proving" herself as it was pursuing something she loved to do for herself. After going to Main for simple battery charges for punching her cousin at age 13, Jada felt as if she disappointed herself and others and did not know how to stop it. "The same day I got out [of Main] my mom picked me up . . . I don't know what happened. I just started going bad. [I was] fighting in school, violating probation, trying to hang out with the wrong crowd and some of the people locked up were my best friends." Jada's self-assessment that she "just started going bad" without being able to provide any further analysis was disconcerting. Her domestic dispute with her cousin seemed to spiral downward; while she had "never been locked up before" it was the beginning of a series of problems. Jada's sense of participation was compelling. Throughout her introspection she imagined what others were thinking or saying about her when they saw her perform, "She's participating in something and trying." The process of reading through plays, learning about characters, memorizing lines, blocking, and preparing for a public performance requires participation. In the chapter, "Performing inoperative community," Rose (1997) explains that process "refers to how participants learn skills and create art when they become involved in a project. . . . Participation entails more of itself. It regenerates itself, and this is its purpose. The process of participation is therefore never quite complete. It is a performance constantly reconstituting itself" (p. 195). For Jada and other girls, participation and the process of participation fed them.

Jada believed that the plays helped her develop problem-solving strategies because "they are real plays" that "real people have [written about] real teenage lives." "By me actually reading these plays," explained Jada, "and doing the plays that actually happened to other people will just make me not even want to go that route. It just caught on—somebody else has been through this. This is how it turned out in the end. This is just somewhere I don't want to go. So I'm gonna' go this way and finish school." Cast in two plays during the summer 2007 program, Jada had opportunities to play a serious role as well as a comedic role. The first play, "True Life," fit into Jada's "real teenage lives" category. Jada played a character named Isis who, according to Jada, "is a girl who wasn't getting along with her mom and dad and ran away from home. She went to stay with a pimp." Jada changed to first person as she described the play and her character specifically, "And I'm trying to figure out how I'm gonna get home because it's not easy to try to leave a pimp. He might try to hit me or kill me. It's not that easy so I'm trying to figure out ways I can get home." With such an intense role, Jada welcomed the comedic relief of "Hair Drama" written by fellow peer Lisa in the summer program. Similar to a scene in George C. Wolf's *The Colored Museum*, "Hair Drama" was a 21st-century rendition of two wigs competing for the attention of a customer in a wig shop. "I'm a wig . . . a classy wig," boasted Jada, "I'm human hair. I'm nice silky human hair." The other wig—"a 70s style puff"—was Wet and Wavy's friend until they both wanted to be chosen by the customer. "So you know how you're friends with somebody and then y'all get in an argument when it comes to getting chosen by somebody?" Jada asked me and then answered before I could respond, "Y'all not so much friends anymore." Jada enjoyed her roles so much—she and her mother decided to include both plays as part of their family reunion activities. Kaya gave them fresh copies of the scripts and Jada enlisted siblings and cousins to perform.

Reading through "Hair Drama" for the first time was a lesson on using context clues for Jada. During he first reading of "Hair Drama," also referred to as a "cold reading" or "table reading," actors are invited by Director Zaire to "stumble through the script." This practice created a relaxing environment and accommodated every reading level. Since Jada was playing the "Wet and Wavy" wig, Zaire asked her to look for clues in the script that would help her create her character. Jada discussed this process in great detail in her interview because she viewed it as one of the most important aspects of Girl Time:

By reading through the play, the first clue it gave me was "Wet and Wavy" was prissy because "Afro Wig" said to her, "Well you think you all that and think you from Hollywood but you was made in Taiwan like the rest of us!" (Interview, June 2007)

Jada was studious and she coveted the idea that she was becoming more skillful in her reading. When Anne led the initial cold readings on the first day of the summer program, she always began with some words of wisdom for the ensemble: "Remember you are word detectives. You are looking for clues throughout the readings—either in the stage direction, the punctuation, or in the words themselves—for clues about how you should shape your character." Zaire's approach was a bit different—when girls read too fast and ignored the punctuation, Zaire would say, "Those periods and commas mean something to me baby!!!" Jada felt more comfortable learning in Girl Time's environment and talked at length about the contrast between her schooling experiences and Girl Time:

[In] regular school . . . they have a group for the kids. A room for the kids, not like a private school. They have like 20-something kids in one class and everybody is acting up so a teacher has got to stop his subject to try to get this kid. Everybody is not getting a clear understanding of the subject . . . I appreciate all the teachers in Girl Time because they take their time with us. Even though we have 7 days, they take their time and they listen and they try their best to help us with what they can. If we need help with our lines they go over it, they go over it, they go over it. They always find a way to make something work. Just like my baby. When my baby had to come 2 days straight, they always found a way to make it work because they didn't want me to miss a day. And I appreciate it. (Interview, June 2007)

There was an inclusive culture when it came to parenting in the Girl Time circle. It is unfair to compare this to a public school where there really are not enough resources to do what Girl Time does; however, I think the mindset that Girl Time teachers maintained with the girls who are mothers worked really well. Girl Time teachers had an unwavering commitment to honor the girls as mothers; they exchanged parenting experiences and I have never observed any finger wagging when it came to teenage pregnancy. The girls come as they are and they have a seat at the table. When Jada returned the following summer of 2008 for the summer program, she had a second son. She completed her GED but was looking for a job. While she began the program with a great deal of enthusiasm, she was also more visibly tired and vocal about their struggles. Returning to Girl Time was a way for her to demonstrate to her boys that she could be a mother and still pursue something she loved. "Acting gives me a lot of confidence . . . and it shows [my sons] that mom is what's up! It shows them that I can still do it and I got two kids but that's not stopping me from doing something that I want to do. A lot of people don't see that." Jada's parents were caring for her first son, and her second son was with his father "temporarily" until Jada could get back on her feet. One day during our "downtime" on our way from the train station to the summer program, Jada talked at length about environment and social class. The conversation went like this:

> *Jada*: Well, in my environment, in my neighborhood, there's
>   not a lot of good things going on over there. There's a lot
>   of drug dealing, and shooting, and fights. And the police
>   over there all the time. [Girl Time] brings you out of that
>   because you being around it and into it, a lot of people say
>   you got your own choices. You do got your own choices,
>   but environment is also important. If you're around it, and
>   you see this stuff every day, it kind of brings you down and
>   you start doing stuff that you know you don't do. It starts
>   off small. For instance, smoking weed. You might not smoke
>   weed, but then you take a little . . . and it just keep coming.
>   Being [in Girl Time] brings me away from all that hoodness
>   and the drama with the police and all the mess going on
>   there. I love being here. It just brings me out into a whole
>   different environment. It's like I'm under a whole new sky or
>   something.
> *Maisha*: I think what you're saying is really powerful . . . I think
>   a lot of times, and you said it, people think, Oh, it's your
>   choice, just don't do it. And I keep hearing people say, "Do
>   the right thing." And then when I ask people what "Do
>   the right thing" means . . . they can tell me everything that
>   you're not supposed to do but they can't say what to do.
>   And then my question has to change to what would have to
>   change around you, in your world. Not just you personally,
>   but what would have to change around your peers for them
>   to be able to do this "right thing?"

Jada: It's about the environment. Even if you have to stay in that environment, you don't have to be around it. And you can go and do something else that ain't around it. And you aren't doing nothing else. And if it's something that you want to do, why not? Why not get away from it? I mean me being there, that gets me into trouble if I'm hanging around those people. Sometimes just sitting and looking at people doing the same stuff every day can be bad for you. I've been in that neighborhood for 17 years. And the same kids from when I first moved over there are doing the same thing. They ain't changed. They ain't doing nothing, still walking up and down the street begging for money, 43 years old staying with their moms. You just get sick of looking at it sometimes. You just want to go somewhere else and do something different. I like being here, it gives me something different to look forward to. (Interview, June 2008)

Jada's observations and analysis of her environment challenged the idea that one had choices. First Jada argued that one's environment made all the difference. Yet, Jada acknowledged that she actively sought to change her environment by attending Girl Time where she was "under a whole new sky." What the other teaching artists and I did not realize at the time I sat down with Jada, we eventually learned she was living in a "trap house" or a drug house during the week of the summer 2008 program. First, she confided in Kaya who quietly asked us for clothing and toiletries for Jada since they kept getting stolen where she was staying. When she showed up to the program in the middle of the week completely disheveled and seemingly disconnected from all of us, we were at a loss for how to support her. Jada accused the teachers of stealing over $100 from her purse and threatened all of us with harm as she called her brother to back her up. I asked her to sit with me for a while so she could calm down and she admitted she really needed somewhere to stay and fell asleep on one of the tables in the multi-service center. We decided as a teaching team that we needed to make some calls and find a place for Jada to stay; however, the calls I made all led to dead ends. I was shocked at how illiterate I was at navigating "the system" and how complicated it was to find a home for this 17-year-old. The only options were going into the custody of the state, and she would have to do so without her children since she was under 18 years of age. The teaching team put our heads together again but at this point Jada woke up and said a few choice words to all of us before making a dramatic exit with her brother, who also called us a few names. One of the probation officers reminded Jada and her brother that they were in a Department of Juvenile Justice facility and would be arrested if they did not leave, which made the situation even more intense. The very system we wanted girls to be liberated from had to step in and navigate an awkward confrontation especially since we had the rest of the girls in the program bearing witness.

Jada had one more year to be in Girl Time and she knew that once she turned 18 we really did not have any other opportunities available to the girls we taught to live freely, laugh freely, create, and build. I wondered if we were giving them false hope or selling a pipe dream that you really could be free. How much freedom does one have in a theatre program by day and a trap house by night? Other than one of the teachers taking Jada into her home—something we all discussed—there were not many options. I saw the same scenarios in schools where I taught; teachers providing transportation, toiletries, lunch money, basics to students out of their own pockets and even taking students in, which solved the problem temporarily. However, many of these loving efforts could not be sustained for many reasons. While I do not think any of the teaching artists will ever get over what happened with Jada, I know that she forced all of us to rethink our role(s) in the girls' lives and to figure out ways to provide extended resources to girls. We did theatre and arts well and we provided a place for girls to perform their possibilities "under a whole new sky"; Jada forced us to reconsider their realities as well. While it took some time, a network was founded one year after this excruciating reminder that our students often needed more than we had to give. I return to the need for coalition building in the fifth and final act; however, it was our experience with Jada that really made us think more about how to pool resources for student artists in the program.

"Real Girls Can Do This": Lisa

"I write my own songs . . . I never thought about writing plays," explained Lisa who was a girl of few words when we first met. Born in the urban southeast in 1992, Lisa was 15 when we met. She was always even, flexible, and calm—a skill she learned as the oldest of six children. Lisa loved to wear dresses and skirts, especially ones with floral patterns. Her hair was always pulled back without one strand out of place. She opened up during downtime but was quiet the rest of the time. On stage one could hardly recognize the resounding voice that came from her petite frame.

Living with her mom, stepfather, and some of her siblings at the time we met, Lisa described a typical day in her life. "People in my neighborhood fight every day . . . they argue. But in my household we don't hardly go outside because they start stuff too much." I first met Lisa in 2006 during a Girl Time workshop at Main. Lisa explained that she was "skipping school" and "running away," but "that's it," when she was arrested. When she learned about Girl Time, she was not initially interested, "This lady asked me if I wanted to do playmaking and I asked, 'What's that?' When I got up there everybody was standing in a circle . . . it was wonderful to see all the faces and just being there."

She was the coauthor of the enormously funny and popular play "Hair Drama." I also met Lisa's mother and one of her younger sisters on the second day of the Main workshop when families are invited to watch the plays. Lisa's mother, Mrs. Luke, was soft-spoken, gracious, and grateful for the work Girl Time did with Lisa. Tempest, Lisa's younger sister, was also impressed with the plays. Lisa was surprised at her own ability to write a play:

> I thought writing a play would be rough because you have to
> [write] lots of lines. I did not know how to do it. I thought it
> was going to be like a story. With Ms. Zaire she told me to write
> in scenes . . . I came up with the title "Hair Drama" because I
> looked around the detention center and everyone's hair was
> messed up and mines was too! (Interview, June 2007)

Mrs. Luke was so struck by watching Lisa perform that she stayed in touch with Kaya until the summer to ensure both Lisa and her younger sister could participate. Even though Lisa's sister, Tempest, had never been involved in the juvenile justice system, Ms. Luke believed she could "learn from the mistakes of others." Tempest became the resident little sister to Girl Time and took pride in "keeping an eye" on her big sister. In the summer 2007 program Lisa was cast in "Ride or Die" as Star, or the "ride or die chick." Described by the playwright Sanaa earlier in this act, Lisa had her own way of describing the play, "'Ride or die' tells about a wife . . . and girlfriend and basically Smoke loves his girlfriend but his wife is just there. The reason Smoke loves Star is because she does things that his wife don't do . . . I play Star and she sends him to jail." I wanted to know more about what Lisa thought about the play and her role as Star:

> *Lisa*: See, Star is a moneymaker. She loves money. Basically that's all she wanted from Smoke was money.
>
> *Maisha*: What does ride or die mean?
>
> *Lisa*: Ride or die means you put yourself in somebody—if you don't ride with them or stick with them they will probably kill you . . . you his chick 'til the end.
>
> *Maisha*: So at the end of the play when Star says, "I was down for the ride but not for the die"—
>
> *Lisa*: Star just lets go of Smoke. Those were strong words . . . it was wrong how she did him because you supposed to be there 'til the end. She lied. Star was wrong. (Interview, June 2007)

Lisa's assessment of Star was part of the surprise and delight many of the teaching artists had when Sanaa wrote the play; teachers were accustomed to girls holding perspectives similar to Lisa's perspective. Star, according to Lisa, promised to be loyal to Smoke yet "just lets go" at the end. For Star and many other girls this was unacceptable because "she lied," regardless if that loyalty had a steep price. When we took this performance back to Main RYDC I sat among incarcerated girls in the audience. During the final scene when Star has the police waiting for Smoke, many of the girls shouted, "She's a snitch! She's wrong!" However, once Star made her powerful declaration it was as if something shifted and the same girls who called out "Snitch!" were equally as moved by Star's movement toward independence. I was also intrigued by the ways in which talking about the plays and Lisa's characters helped her open up during the interview. Many of her responses prior to discussing the play were short sentences and she often responded, "Can't say." At one point we stopped the formal interview and talked through the process because I wanted to be sure she was comfortable.

When Lisa and I sat down again in the summer of 2008 she was 16 and in the 11th grade. Expecting a baby boy (due any day after the summer program ended), Lisa was already thinking about what she would teach her son. "I'm gonna tell my son about life because I know I been through it with the rape and all that. [I'm gonna teach him] how to treat women." When Lisa mentioned she had been raped I was unprepared; she had not disclosed this before, yet, mentioned it as if I knew. Lisa retraced the steps leading to her incarceration, and it was evident that she was running away and that skipping school was her response to the sexual, physical, and mental abuse she had been experiencing. Returning to the Girl Time ensemble for a second year was an affirming choice for Lisa:

> I like acting and you get to take your feelings out and tell real
> stories like where I've been in life. And you can tell people
> what's really going on in life. You can tell them your stories . . .
> I'm getting a lot out of Girl Time now that I am where I should
> be . . . I read poems to learn what happened to people and songs
> . . . Real girls can do this. (Interview, June 2008)

Knowing that "real girls" could write plays, poetry, and perform them as well helped Lisa understand that she was in a welcoming space. Writing, creativity, and participation were exclusive, or reserved for a particular kind of girl. Real girls—according to Lisa—with real life issues could also be affirmed through their work. I initially thought that girls who were in the process of becoming mothers, or even girls who were already mothers, would not have time or make time for Girl Time; however, the mothers and mothers-to-be like Lisa seemed to need the program more than anyone. In Girl Time, these young mothers had a chance to do something for themselves, build relationships with a community of women, and simply play.

Lisa and I reflected on "Ride or Die" from the year before when we sat down in 2008 when she asserted, "Something real like that can happen, you know?" In summer 2009, Lisa returned and was focused on being "happy" and "having fun." Now an 11th-grader with a 1-year-old son, Lisa had more to say about being a girl and developing a sense of self:

> You've gotta have respect and confidence about yourself. Knowing that you can do it. Never say that you can't. You can always
> achieve. Motivation and have a lot of courage and you can do
> it . . . Like when a boy walks up to me I have more respect for
> myself as a lady. Like I tell them no. I am not going to go up to
> the house with you, no. I just walk away from the situation.
> (Interview, June 2009)

Lisa fiercely believed that girls needed people they could go to for "advice," and Lisa used the Girl Time teaching artist network much more between the summer 2008 and summer 2009 program than she had the previous year. She also saw that she enjoyed acting in comedies and playing nonhuman characters. This gave her an opportunity to stretch herself and leave some of the real-life issues behind for a moment in time.

"I Just Want to See Everything": Janelle

"I write . . . poetry. Well, I really don't call it poetry but I put what I been through without saying it or without telling the whole story. I write poems and write them on my MySpace page." All of the teaching artists met Janelle during the summer 2008 program. Kaya invited Janelle to participate in Girl Time after a chance encounter at Home Depot. Always in Girl Time mode, Kaya approached Janelle and her mother with a flyer inviting them to the summer 2008 performance. However, Janelle had alternative plans; rather than sit in the audience she wanted to be on the stage. After talking it over, Janelle's mother agreed. As it turned out Girl Time would become an important tool for Janelle, who had moved to the urban southeast from the Midwest only 7 months prior to meeting Kaya. "The culture is different here," Janelle explained, "in the Midwest I would be the only African American girl in the class. Here I go to school and there's only one Caucasian person. It's different. It's kinda rough at first because I want to get out and see things. This place is huge so I want to see everything and I kind of get in trouble here and there."

Janelle struggled with the ensemble—she was obsessed with other peoples' skin and hair and asked lots of questions about ethnic identity. I sat next to Janelle on our first day of the summer 2008 program. "Are you mixed?" she asked crudely while staring at my hair. Zaire, who was within earshot offered, "Yeah, mixed up and crazy like the rest of us." We all laughed. Janelle refused to be completely distracted and continued, "You have pretty hair, I love it." I repeated a quote I heard the poet Aya de Leon tell one of my Bronx student poets after a reading in New York City years ago, "Thank you but I need you to love your own hair. There was a time when I didn't like mine." This encounter reminded me of Ward's (2000) study of African American parents "raising resisters," in which she opened her study with an account of a mother describing how she taught her daughter to touch and feel her tightly curled hair and recognize how pretty it was. Ward argues that this mother's story was a "unique psychological script" guided by the mother's sense that her daughter would eventually experience "the attacks on her self-esteem by those who measure her beauty against a White standard and devalue her Blackness and self-worth" (p. 50). Janelle had yet to become a "resister," but she would eventually use the Girl Time process to begin the work of becoming one.

Part of Janelle's social awkwardness was she had been moving between detention centers and foster homes prior to moving to the southeast. "Right now, I'm in no grade. I was in foster care for 5 years, so when I moved around a lot school got put on hold. So right now I'm supposed to be a senior and I'm a freshman . . . they told me I'm gonna have to try other options." I was unable to verify what grade Janelle was supposed to be in, but I did learn that she was missing too many units to complete a traditional journey to a high school diploma. Janelle was feeling the push and pull of being the interesting new girl yet being regarded with skepticism. She was fashion forward and making her own clothing, which garnered even more attention. Janelle was eager to have a venue for her energy:

> I'm always acting silly and I'm always just doing crazy stuff . . .
> I always wanted to [act]. So when I met Kaya . . . I just asked if
> there was anyway I could be in the play . . . When she told me
> the program was for girls who had been in detention centers I
> had sympathy because I've been in that situation and know what
> it's like. And when people are like, "Oh, those girls are in deten-
> tion, I don't want no part of it," I know it's not always their fault.
> (Interview, June 2008)

It was a coincidence that this girl strolling through the aisles of Home Depot would need Girl Time at this point in her life. So Kaya and Janelle became close. Janelle talked to me about how she viewed her participation in Girl Time: "I'm building self-esteem and courage. I'm learning confidence. If I have something to say . . . I don't sit there in a corner. Be able to speak your mind and when you say it—say it strong and confidently." Perhaps even more important, Janelle used Girl Time to work through her struggles getting along with other girls, "One thing I'm getting from the program is being with a room a full of females and not arguing. That is good for me. I can take that back to school."

Janelle was cast in three plays during her first summer. In "Hi, My Name Is Mariah," she played a woman in an Alcoholics Anonymous meeting offering to help a new member. Her second role was in "Where to Turn," playing a 13-year-old runaway who confesses her pregnancy to her father. When her father gets angry she runs away and can only find work as a stripper and a prostitute. "I'm not gonna lie," said Janelle, "I can't connect to this character at all." However in "To Bully or not to Bully," in which Janelle played a victim of bullying, she initially felt a connection to the bully:

> I relate to the bully because she don't got no one there and I
> got put in foster care. Although it would look like my mother

left me, she didn't. She did it to help me because I was getting abused and she wanted to help me. And if I had to, I wouldn't take none of it back. What I went through made me who I am today. If I didn't go through those I would just be in denial about life and kind of stuck up. (Interview, June 2008)

Our time together took an unexpected turn. As Janelle asserted how much she had in common with the bully, she decided that it was the bullying victim whose experiences she shared more:

I been bullied a lot in my life. When I moved down here, everything was good. In the [Midwest] there were not a lot of dark-skinned girls so I got picked on a lot about that. And now I'm down here and my mom is helping me with my self-esteem. It's hard now. It was hard then. (Interview, June 2008)

We stopped the interview; Janelle was sobbing and the posturing and tough exterior she used as a shield all week began to dissipate. We sat for a while talking about the pressures associated with skin tone and hair texture. We exchanged our own war stories about "good hair/bad hair" and "light skin/dark skin" that we encountered. It was an unfortunate Black girl rite of passage, but what saved me was having parents with Black Nationalist ideologies who pumped "Black is Beautiful" into my veins to prepare me for the moments that Janelle had to confront often unarmed and vulnerable. I was able to talk to the teaching artists so that they could get a clearer understanding of Janelle's struggles, and Zaire pledged to work more closely with Janelle.

When the summer 2008 program went on the road to the detention centers, Janelle came apart on stage during "To Bully or not to Bully." Convinced that her fellow ensemble member, Megan, was masquerading behind her role as the bully, Janelle believed Megan really pulled her hair (during a scene in the play) on purpose. "Stage combat," the art of creating violent scenes on the theatre stage, was an important part of the Girl Time teaching. In stage combat "the victim is always in control of the movement" explained Kaya. From Janelle's perspective, Megan took advantage and pulled a little too hard. Janelle cursed Megan on the make-shift stage (the front of a recreation room) and stormed off. In this paralyzing moment, a DJJ counselor and Kaya sat with Janelle trying to calm her and work through everything. Girls in the audience did not laugh or find any joy in what they witnessed but seemed to have empathy with the cast. The other teaching artists moved the show along and stepped in for Janelle's roles. At this point, the old school Girl Time student artists, Nia, Lisa, and Tempest wanted to support Janelle. Nearly everyone had a different version of what happened, when and how it started, but we all understood that we needed additional support. The incident with Jada had taken place earlier that week so we were engaged in the process of finding counselors and social workers to be a part of the teaching team. Much like Rhodessa Jones' work with The Medea Project, we knew we could not do this work alone. Jones' co-teacher, Sean Reynolds, was a seasoned social worker and the two complemented each other. Janelle's life for the next year was a series of twists and turns. Zaire obtained temporary custody of Janelle after sitting and talking to her mother. When Janelle returned for the summer 2009 program she walked taller, seemed more self-assured, and positioned herself as a leader among the girls.

Janelle was able to talk through the previous year, which ended in her being disrespectful to Kaya who had invited her to participate in the program in the first place. Kaya was clear that she wanted to give Janelle a second chance and believed there was more for Janelle and all of the teaching artists to learn by continuing to work together than not. Janelle recalled:

> When I got the phone call—well actually when [the month of] May came around and I realized that Girl Time was starting to come up, I got nervous because last year when I didn't get along with Kaya and had the big altercation, I didn't think Girl Time would want me back, but when I got the phone call from Kaya, I was excited. I appreciate that a lot. (Interview, June 2009)

Kaya reached out to Janelle to underscore the program's commitment to her personal growth and development. Janelle was talented—she could act, sing, and dance, and when she wanted to organize and inspire others she was capable of doing that as well. Janelle explained that Zaire had been teaching her how to "love myself" and process the previous year. "I learned to always keep my composure," Janelle shared and we both smiled widely. "[I learned] to be more confident and accepting me for who I am. And not trying to change myself for other people to accept or like me," Janelle explained. However, it was the ensemble of teaching artists constantly checking in and creating a safety net around Janelle that may have helped facilitate this process. According to Janelle,

[Girl Time] teachers get more one-on-one with you. They get to know you. It's not even as if they're just teachers teaching a class to get paid. [Teachers] are here because they want you to learn, "I want you to take this experience and use it in life." They are accepting. They accept you however you come. And in school, I've learned that teachers don't care if we succeed or fail because they already have their education and it wouldn't hurt them because at the end of the night they go home. And it's just, you get more of a connection in Girl Time. (Interview, June 2009)

Layli, the theatre stage manager, recognized Janelle's talent and offered her a scholarship to the theatre program she orchestrated that took place after Girl Time's program was over. Layli's program cost over $2000, and she gave a scholarship every year to a Girl Time ensemble member. In spite of the conflict that had occurred, Layli offered and Janelle accepted, which also helped Janelle become determined to work on her sense of self.

Discussion

When I invited Janelle to interview me, she asked "What made you decide to get into working with teenage girls who have been in like Main RYDC . . . what made you give these girls the opportunity?" I think the question she asked in many ways reflected her surprise that the teaching artists would welcome her back and give her a fresh beginning. This discourse of second chances was not discussed explicitly by teaching artists but it was practiced. Teaching artists willingly shared their flaws and uninformed decisions and left an open space for exchanging stories through discussing plays, characters, and themes. Student artists did not have to go through a hazing process for acceptance. Girls came as they were and made decisions about what they wanted to discard as well as what they desired to carry away.

In the next act, I examine literature on the school-to-prison pipeline, with a focus on how girls have been impacted by the gendering of youth justice. This departure from narratives of student and teaching artists is an effort to present the issues, now that you have met the girls and women whose lives have been significantly impacted by particular policies and practices.

The Trouble with Black Girls

Racing, Classing, and Gendering the School-to-Prison Pipeline

Walking into the multi-service center where the Girl Time summer program is held, we pass through a seemingly inconsistent metal detector. When it goes off no one really takes notice and these days it may as well be unplugged. A large sign that reads, "Welcome" is hung above another poster reading "The Road to Good Character." While it is unclear where this road begins and exactly where it goes, a nearby table full of brochures about abstinence only until marriage suggests that this could be one of the first stops. An African American woman behind the counter offers a warm smile and gestures to us that we need to sign the visitors log. Before we can turn the corner into the room where we begin our workshops with a donated dinner from community members, board members, and collaborators, there is another sign reading, "You are responsible for your own actions." This is the building that houses probation officers serving youth who have been released from detention centers. I have never seen a White person in this building with the exception of a few of the Girl Time teachers: youth, probation officers, and administrators are all Black. Relationships between POs and girls look familial from the outside looking in; POs volunteer to hold babies, observe workshops, and offer smiles that you can't resist returning. Girls run to embrace the POs they have not seen in a long time, while the POs express their joy that there has been a lapse in contact, because it means the girls are "staying out of trouble."

Although the building is nondescript and in serious need of fresh paint, new flooring, and an overhaul of the air conditioning unit, each office is decorated to match the personalities of the employees who occupy them. In sum, they are doing their best to change the aesthetics of the building with their small contributions. Our meeting room is a prime example of neglected buildings housing youth in urban areas and the people who work with them. Sometimes hotter than outside, the recreation room looks more like a picked over yard sale—a Ping Pong table is pushed in the corner while a cemetery of office furniture occupies another. Vending machines that enjoy taking more than giving only offer snacks high in sugar, fat, and salt. Military posters haphazardly hang on a few walls and a lone bulletin board, perhaps the second stop on the "Road to Good Character," reads "The Garden of Good Character." Faded construction paper cut carefully into the shapes of flowers—tulips, daffodils, and roses with long green stems and leaves attached in certain places suggesting a 3-D effect. At the foot of this flowerbed reads, "How does your garden grow?" Each stem offers an answer: persistence, honesty, courage, charity, responsibility, poise, purpose, diligence, justice, achievement, love, life, integrity, caring, respect, success, citizenship, fairness, strength, and confidence.

At first glance these posters and bulletins conjure images of affirmation. Few would argue that love, life, and integrity as well as other "flowers" in the so-called "garden of good character" are not important in young lives. In the context of this space—a Department of Juvenile Justice multiservice center, housing probation officers serving formerly incarcerated youth, and the home of the Girl Time summer program—these messages assume that a lack of character or a lapse in character is why most of the young people are in this building in the first place. These messages—implicitly and explicitly—encapsulate what the world has come to think about youth, and girls in particular. Some of the implicit messages can be read in the walls of this decaying building; any effort to make it more stimulating is because the men and women who work there use their own resources. Simply put, the POs are doing the best they can, and, like many teachers working in undesirable conditions, this community is trying to do so with as much grace as they can muster. In spite of their efforts, this building still sends a message that urban youth are undeserving and unworthy of a second chance. From the lack of healthy snacks or eateries in the area, to the focus on "character" (abstinence), every wall, poster, and brochure translates into "You are here because you messed up and now you have to fix it." If one were to read the walls in this building, the only "fix" along the road to good character besides abstaining would be to join the military. Sometimes I would get to the facility early enough to read through some of the "do it yourself" brochures and one very out of place Suzanne Somers book, *Breakthrough: Eight Steps to Wellness* (with a close shot of the very blond and very fair Somers who did not resemble anyone who came into the building), that sat on the coffee table in the waiting area. I often wondered to myself and aloud to anyone who would listen if it were possible for the young people who entered this building to grow their garden of good character. Would they be given another chance to redefine themselves beyond the labels that clung to them mercilessly or would they always be imprisoned by some of their past actions?

The purpose of Act IV is to interrogate the literature that intersects education, literacy, and school-to-prison pipeline issues. Here I seek to examine these studies through the lens of gender to complicate the school-to-prison pipeline, that is, the ushering of particular students from schools to detention centers, jails, and prisons through miseducation, suspensions, expulsions, zero-tolerance practices, and "diploma denial" (Fine & Ruglis, 2009). This interdisciplinary approach to reviewing literature is at once strategic and purposeful. First, I wish to introduce various stakeholders, such as, middle school and high school (although the pipeline can begin much earlier than this) teachers, school staff (including school security and assistant principals of "discipline"), administrators, teacher educators, and those who either create or impact policies concerning urban youth, through an examination of the school-to-prison pipeline literature. In Act V, I will invite the same stakeholders to imagine alternatives to zero-tolerance policies and practices in schools that focus on roles as opposed to relationships. Next, in this Act I specifically examine the ways in which Black girls have become the victims of such policies and have been omitted from social science research. Throughout Act IV, I continue to call on the stories and experiences of Nia, Sanaa, Lisa, Jada, and Janelle, as well as other formerly incarcerated girls, in the hope that the ideas presented in this Act can be used to stimulate dialogue among people who work directly with teen girls and/or make decisions that can offer positive influences in their lives.

The Road to Good Character or Another Dead End?

The so-called road to good character is part and parcel of what Fine and Ruglis (2009) refer to as the "discourse of personal responsibility" (p. 20). Through this discourse, Black and Brown youth learn they are unworthy and undeserving of a critical education through the process of "dispossession" or the taking away of a "universal right" (education and literacy) and making this right something that must be earned through academic achievement and test performance, in spite of a trajectory of miseducation and "diploma denial" (Ruglis, 2010; Winn & Behizadeh, in press). When poor students of color do not perform well in schools, they are led to believe that this public failure is indeed a private matter. Cloaked in shame and failure, poor students of color are often unable to recognize they have been subjected to "urban pedagogies" (Duncan, 2000). According to Duncan, urban pedagogies "work through and upon adolescents of color" by focusing on "discipline and control," as opposed to "intellectual rigor and the development of meaningful skills" (p. 30). Due to a lack of robust learning opportunities, many youth of color do not develop the critical literacy skills that would enable them to critique their own experiences. A culture of incarceration, which can begin early in schools and communities, "requires that the experiences and the lives of those harmed by institutions and policies be transformed from concrete, potentially revolutionary, evidence into private, individual failures" (Meiners, 2007, p. 140). In sum, many youth begin to think that dropping out, failure, and even incarceration are a part of their life cycle or even a warped rite of passage. As the stakes for public schools get higher, particular youth are ushered into what has been referred to as the school-to-prison pipeline,[1] and for some children, this process begins earlier in what is known as the "cradle to prison pipeline" (Children's Defense Fund, 2007). Fine and Ruglis (2009) acknowledge how practices contributing to this school/prison nexus are central to dispossession in the lives of poor youth of color in urban public schools:

> There is perhaps no more vivid illustration of accumulation by dispossession than policy that infuse public schools with criminal justice surveillance, literally sucking out time, resources, relationships and space from teaching and learning, redirecting these resources into criminal surveillance and pursuit. (p. 21)

In fact students often learn to do time before they even set foot in a detention center, jail, or prison (McGrew, 2007). "Education's prisoners," according to McGrew, are youth attending "the armed camps that many of our nation's schools are becoming [which illuminates] the growing relationship between schooling, the political economy, and the prison industrial complex" (p. 19). This notion of *ghetto schooling* relegates youth in poor, underserved communities to schools that promote discipline and control over robust teaching and learning opportunities (Anyon, 1997). Both students and teachers become imprisoned by the idea that Black and Brown bodies are in need of constant policing and surveillance, and that youth should seldom, if ever, be heard. Students of color feel the impact of the school/prison nexus more than any other group:

> Trapped in failing schools that are often physically deteriorating, disciplined and moved into juvenile justice systems through violations of punitive zero tolerance policies, failing to pass high stakes standardized tests and channeled into special education programs, youth of color are, materially and conceptually moved from schools to jails. (Meiners, 2007, p. 16)

Meiners names and points fingers at the many contributors to this pipeline; however, one of the key components of the school-to-prison pipeline is what has been referred to as the "discipline gap" (Gregory, Skiba, & Noguera, 2010). In her presidential address to the American Educational Research Association annual meeting in 2006, Gloria Ladson-Billings offered a new lens through which to view America's achievement gap. The "education debt," argued Ladson-Billings was at the foundation of the gap and a debt that was owed to American Indian, African American, and Latino students in urban public schools. Documenting the legacy of denying equality in education and miseducation throughout America's history, Ladson-Billings asserted that until these debts are paid in full, education will continue to see disparities in achievement. This debt now looms over the ways in which urban schools handle conflict in schools.

Gregory, Skiba, and Noguera (2010) analyze racial disparity in achievement and its relationship to discipline and, more specifically, suspensions in schools. Black, Latino, and American Indian students encounter more discipline sanctions in schools than their White counterparts. These discipline sanctions typically equate to missed instruction and engagement with teachers and peers. In fact, Gregory and her colleagues posit,

"The school disciplinary practices used most widely throughout the United States may be contributing to lowered academic performance among the group of students in greatest need of improvement" (p. 60). Scholarship examining the achievement gap has also argued that it is "a mirror image to the punishment gap" (Yang, 2009, p. 49). In a study revisiting the concepts of discipline and punishment, Yang (2009) challenges educators and administrators to interrogate their so-called discipline strategies. "Crudely speaking," asserts Yang, "more discipline should result in more achievement" (p. 51). According to the Advancement Project, a working group organized by the Civil Rights Project at Harvard University, only 26 states "require alternative education assignments for students who are suspended or expelled" (The Advancement Project, 2000, p. vii). Therefore, most students who are suspended never receive course work or instruction, sending their academic careers into a downward spiral.

Throughout this process, youth who do not fit into a middle class, status quo profile are constructed as "public enemies" (Meiners, 2007). Through the process of "ideological management," argues Meiners, "schools normalize particular family structures," or ways of being and knowing, often distinguishing between "who is in need and worthy of state protection" and "what and who is to be feared" (Meiners, p. 5). Nia's narrative in Act III captured the process through which youth experience being constructed as a public enemy. For Nia, the institutional restrictions of both foster care and school were homophobic and stifling. From the foster home where she was "discovered" as gay that called her mom to "tell on her," to the boy at school who accused her of "turning his sister gay," there was a heteronormative script that she veered from and consequently was punished for not following. School security and the juvenile courtroom contributed to this process; the unidentified people in the courtroom, who painted a picture of Nia as a repeat offender with no hopes of doing anything positive, did not know the Nia who would become a leader in a community of student artists, learn how to build ensemble with girls and women, and perform lived experiences on stages. Fine and Ruglis (2009) further argue that "educators, parents, and youth try to negotiate conditions of systematic miseducation and the scientism of high-stakes testing, while ideologies about merit, deservingness, and blame drip feed into the soul, tagging some bodies as worthy and others as damaged" (p. 20–21). Again, Nia's narrative demonstrated the ways in which youth experience dispossession. Nia never learned the names of the male security who searched her or even questioned the problems with male security personnel searching female students. Nia and her mother did not have an opportunity to meet with the school administrators (nor did they demand one), in spite of her teachers writing letters of support on her behalf. And this dispossession continued in juvenile court where Nia encountered individuals who were "for" or "against" her but did not know or understand their particular roles and titles. According to the NAACP Legal Defense Fund (2005), the school-to-prison pipeline is "one of the most urgent challenges in education today." This hybrid of "punitive and overzealous tools and approaches of modern criminal justice system have seeped into our schools, serving to remove children from mainstream education environments and funnel them on to a one-way path to prison." Now this pipeline increasingly threatens the lives of girls, and Black girls in particular.

Sugar and Spice: The Remix

Girls currently account for one in four juvenile arrests in the United States (Dohrn, 2000; Office of Juvenile Justice and Delinquency Prevention [OJJ-DP], 2008). A change in policy regarding status offenses has contributed to the increase in girls being arrested and detained. Status offenses include running away—which was one of the reasons most Girl Time participants cited for their incarceration—as well as truancy and violations of liquor laws. Chesney-Lind (1999) found that, not only did status offenses account for 23.4 arrests of girls in 1995, but more than half of these arrests were for running way from home. Simkins, Hirsch, Horvat, and Moss (2004) assert that "there is evidence that girls are being detained for less serious offenses" (p. 56–57) than their male counterparts. To be frank, girls are reported as runaways more frequently than boys. In this same study, Simkins and her colleagues assert that incarcerated girls report "a high incidence of mother-daughter conflict" (thus leading to offenses such as running way). And while girls have lower recidivism rates, something teaching artists saw in the Girl Time program, they often return to detention centers due to violation of probation. Once released from detention, girls often return to the same problems they faced prior to being incarcerated. The last, and perhaps least surprising, finding from the Simkins study of the school-to-prison pipeline for girls is that once they are incarcerated "there is a paucity of gender-appropriate disposition alternatives to meet the girls' needs" (p. 57). In sum, "gender neutral" or equal opportunity punishment underscoring parity treat women offenders "as if they were men" (Covington & Bloom, 2003). Girls and women do have different needs than boys and men; one of the most obvious is the need for reproductive health education and support.

While the Juvenile Justice and Delinquency Prevention Act in 1974 was created to keep youth accused of status offenses out of detention centers and youth prisons, the period between 1987 and 1996 saw a rise in these offenses being repackaged and renamed, coinciding with more stringent drug laws. Drug laws—like the one that led to Kemba Smith's arrest (see the prologue) are largely to blame for this increase. Bloom (2003) asserts, "the increased incarceration of women appears to be the outcome of larger forces [that] have shaped the U.S. crime policy" (p. 4). Again, Bloom reveals the movement from the context of how girls and women—to borrow Richie's words—are "compelled to crime" to personalizing larger social issues.

In "Look Out Kid, It's Something You Did," Dohrn (2000) asserts that media depictions of an increasingly violent youth are not supported in the data. The Office of Juvenile Justice and Delinquency Prevention (OJJDP) launched the "Girls Study Group" in order to understand and respond to "a surge of girl arrests" that, according to the group, took place during the 1990s. According to OJJDP, "by 2004 females made up 25% of all juvenile arrests for aggravated assault, and 33% of juvenile arrests for other assaults" (OJJDP, 2008, p. 4). However, in spite of this increase in arrests, there was no empirical evidence supporting that girls' behavior had dramatically changed. Indeed, talk shows depicting girl fights and asking why girls have "gone wild" or how they became "worse than boys" began to flood the television airwaves. YouTube videos capturing girl fights were being uploaded and viewed a record number of times and sometimes were even featured on the national news.

While OJJDP maintained that girls did not suddenly become more violent overnight, it asserted that there were possible explanations for the increase of girls' arrests much like the Simkins study. The first possible explanation was that law enforcement policies changed and became more stringent, like those policies impacting drug laws. For example, domestic disputes were being classified as simple assault. In Jada's narrative in Act III, she explained that she was initially arrested for hitting her cousin whom she claimed was harassing her while she was on the phone in her home. While this would have typically been a domestic dispute, police arrested Jada for simple assault, although Jada said the police appeared almost apologetic for having to arrest her for this particular incident. Zero-tolerance policies, according to OJJDP, could also be potential factors in the increased arrests of girls. For example, once Sanaa was a part of the juvenile justice system, she was subject to more restrictions both in and out of school. Skipping school became a violation in probation and resulted in arrest and detention. Another Girl Time student artist, Viola, shared with me how one violation quickly led to others:

> The first time I got locked up, they gave me probation and put me under house arrest. The second time I got real mad at my momma and didn't want to be in the same room with her and the same house with her. So I just left and I was gone for over 24 hours so I was charged as a runaway. Then I cut off my ankle bracelet as well, then I got locked up. I got scared. I thought it would help them track me down . . . But I didn't know so I cut it off. (Interview, June 2008)

Unfortunately, incarcerating youth for truancy typically exacerbates the problem. Rather than creating an intervention, Viola was funneled into the juvenile justice system where one offense led to another until she was released into the custody of a group home.

Foster children often find themselves trapped in a gulf between their foster homes and emancipation; child welfare systems can terminate youth from the foster care system even when youth do not have any viable options (Dohrn, 2000):

> While wardship can continue past 19 upon a showing of "good cause," there is a significant disagreement among child welfare agencies and advocates as to what is meant by "good cause" . . . this extraordinary triage of tens of thousands of youth [who] are, by definition, victims of adult violence, creates a pool of youngsters with slender preparation for higher education, living wage employment or stable family life. (p. 166)

For Janelle, moving from one foster care home to another made school a low priority, while it was replaced by survival. Home for Janelle became a pastiche of foster care homes and detention centers. After Janelle's first summer with Girl Time, her mother "kicked her out," and teaching artists learned just how difficult it was to find resources for girls who were essentially homeless and no longer eligible for foster care. After an exasperating search for resources, Zaire felt she could wait no longer and received temporary guardianship over Janelle. If Zaire had not stepped in to help Janelle navigate the system, I think it would have been likely for Janelle to have gotten entangled with the juvenile justice system again. Few resources were within reach even with someone like Zaire conducting the research.

One of the most terrifying statistics that emerges from studies of incarcerated and formerly incarcerated girls is the number of girls who have encountered sexual abuse (Belknap, 2001; Chesney-Lind, 1997; Fine & McClelland, 2006; Richie, 2005; Simkins, Hirsch, Horvat, & Moss, 2004). "The crime-processing system and society as a whole," argues Belknap, "tend to minimize female victims of male violence, and this is particularly true if the victims are of color and/or poor" (Belknap, 2001, p. 219). In the context of Girl Time, many girls reported being sexually abused and/or raped and cited this abuse as one of the main reasons they chose to run away. Jada offered sage wisdom about this in her summer 2008 interview:

> I really don't think a lot of the girls should be locked up because some of the stuff they do—it's just not worth it. I mean some girls may need to be talked to or some of them do stuff for love or they do stuff to get attention and all this because they don't have it. Then when they do it all of a sudden they are criminals. "Oh well, she need to be locked up because she did this." Talk to them. See what's going on or try to see the whole picture before you just go, "Well you're a criminal, you deserve to be locked up and here's your record. This is what you did and it is what it is." I don't think that's right. A lot of people in the big jails . . . now some people need to be there . . . but a lot I think that they need a second chance. (Interview, June 2008)

Seeing the whole picture meant asking difficult questions about why girls were running away in the first place as well as why girls were skipping school and risking being declared truants. Out of all of the girls I interviewed—all African-American—not one discussed race. It was as if they did not think twice that they were surrounded by girls just like them. A consistent finding in studies of girls of the school-to-prison pipeline is that African American girls are subject to arrests, charges, and incarceration more than any other group. African-Americans account for 50% of girls and women in detention centers, jails, and prisons, whereas, Whites account for 34% and Latina account for 13% (Belknap, 2001, p. 168). The rearview mirror theory, which I discussed briefly in Act II, did not apply for Black and Latino girls. Whereas Ginger's mother was able to talk school authorities out of creating a paper trail for Ginger with suspensions and expulsions and, most importantly, to keep law enforcement out of the conflict, this was not the reality for Black girls in Girl Time, nor is it the reality for Black girls entangled with the system in general. When the Pew Center for the States released its report "One in 100 Americans Behind Bars 2008," not only did it confirm America's reputation as an incarceration nation, but it also revealed that currently 1 in 100 Black women are behind bars as well. In fact, America is not the only country responsible for incarcerating women of color; scholars have argued that a "global lockdown" of women has also ensued (Sudbury, 2005). This global lockdown of women of color has trickled down to girls of color as well. Fine and McClelland (2006) assert:

> As a form of social control on girls, and disproportionately Black and Latino girls, juvenile detention fails to remedy the original problems and serves instead to criminalize and diminish the educational, economic, and health outcomes of young women. (p. 304)

Black girls face more severe punishment than their peers. According to Poe-Yamagata and Jones (2000), 70% of cases involving White girls are dismissed, compared to only 30% of cases involving Black girls. Additionally, Black girls (like Black boys) are more likely to be waived to adult facilities.[2]

The Trouble with Black Girls

Noguera's (2008) compelling scholarship examining "the trouble with black boys" challenges the ways in which Black boys are viewed in education. Responding to the boy crisis, and Black boys in particular, education research has created an agenda examining issues that contribute to Black boys' underperformance in American public schools. Scholars have also challenged this notion of Black children failing by focusing on the ways in which schools have failed them (Irvine, 1990). As a result of the effort to understand the issues that negatively impact Black boys in schools and communities, the construction of Black boys as troubled and in need of intervention has become an uncontested trope (Brown & Brown, 2006). While this book is not a contest or battle of the sexes over which gender struggles more, much of the discourse on boys has overshadowed the ways in which Black girls, too, struggle in schools, communities, and now the juvenile justice system. The "boys in the hood" era—an all too familiar reality for many Black boys throughout the United States—ignored the plight of Black girls. In her work with incarcerated women, Rhodessa

Jones started seeing the inmates get younger and younger in the jail system. "When I saw the film *Boyz in the Hood*," offered Jones, "I thought it was great but I thought, 'What about the girls in the hood? What about us?'"(Jones quoted in Fraden, 2001, p. 91). In the previous acts, and Act III in particular, girls spoke openly about their challenges both in schools and in out-of-school contexts. These voices—the voices of formerly incarcerated girls all of whom are African American—are seldom, if ever, heard in educational research (Paul, 2003). Even as I researched a home for this study, few were brave enough to even consider publishing a book that examined the gendering of the school-to-prison pipeline, especially since Black girls' stories were front and center. In a chapter entitled, "All the Girls are White, all the Boys are Black, but Some of us are Brave" (Paul, 2003, p. 25), Paul argues that as far back as 30 years ago, scholars noted the marginalization of the Black girl experience in social science research:

> One of the great struggles that arise when documenting the early expertise of black girls in schools is that they have not been the focus on the agenda of social science research. . . . Their shadowy status in the literature is a reflection of a more general cultural orientation towards young Black girls. (Lightfoot in Paul, p. 26)

Paul further asserts that elementary age Black girls "interact less frequently with their White female teachers than do their White counterparts, and they are more apt to be ignored . . . usually, the positive feedback young Black girls receive focused on social rather than academic skills and assisting teachers with nonacademic tasks" (Paul, 2003, p. 33). Black girls are the consummate helpers; they often assume administrative roles in the classroom or are put in charge of organizing and managing other students. This caretaker role does little to develop their intellectual habits of mind. When Black girls "talk-back," they are often constructed as loud troublemakers. Media portrayals and a character assassination of Black women depicting them as welfare queens or hypersexualized video vixens has only created more tensions for Black girls. Some Black girls maintain a misunderstood silence or the opposite of talking back as a tool of resistance and survival:

> The particular ways in which Black girls speak, whether loud or silent . . . is often interpreted as disruptive, not as exposing "the view from above." So what happens? Black girls are told by adults who aren't raised to understand or never took the time to learn the nuanced implication of

demanding Black girls to "shut up or speak" and therefore disregard that they have already spoken (or not) and communicated what they need to say. But, it's a no-win situation for the Black girl who is immediately labeled the troublemaker, or the adult who did the labeling. (Brown, 2009, p. 28)

The omission of Black girls' voices, stories, and experiences with schools and now the juvenile justice system is pervasive in educational research; however, there is emerging scholarship seeking to re-center these important voices (Brown, 2009; Evans-Winters, 2005). In the aforementioned study, "Raising Resisters," Ward (2000) revisits research on the psychological development of girls. Like Paul's scholarship, Ward acknowledges that this work has been centered on White girls. Carole Gilligan's works have been, perhaps, some of the most influential in this area: "Brown and Gilligan identify self silence and taking one's knowledge underground as among the costly strategies girls employ to remain accepted by others," begins Ward (p. 53). However, Ward further argues, "This silence provides a frightening illustration of women's response to and capitulation in the face of a patriarchal culture that demands compliance to conventions of femininity. Self-silencing, however may have different motives and consequences for Black adolescent girls" (p. 53).

While some believe that girls and women who commit crimes are rebelling willingly against the status quo and refusing to adhere to heteronormative standards, Richie (1996) asserts, "For some women . . . nonconformity with mainstream is not a privileged position or viable option" (p. 3). In fact, some girls and women are committing crimes to fit in and be accepted and this is especially the case for Black girls in Girl Time; some wanted love and acceptance, while others longed for partnership or companionship. I would argue that the "ride or die" concept is another example of the ways in which incarcerated and formerly incarcerated girls live lives that are "betwixt and between," or consumed by a liminal state, in which they are walking a tightrope between freedom and enslavement; voice and silence; choices and consequences (Winn, 2010b). This push/pull predicament, according to Richie, is even more complicated for incarcerated African American women because it "leaves them facing complicated ethical, moral, and practical dilemmas. The women feel pushed and pulled by their basic survival needs, their expectations of themselves and others' requirements" (Richie, 1996, p. 4).

While Richie's work on "gender entrapment" focuses on the ways in which African American battered women are often "compelled to crime"

(Richie, 1996, p. 4), she also examines the increasing number of Black girls being incarcerated (Richie, 2005). Richie argues that "there is no new crime wave among black girls," yet they are "quickly becoming one of the fastest growing cohorts of incarcerated people in this country" (Richie, 2005, p. 76). Richie further posits, "Despite the image that has been constructed of them, girls in jails, prisons, and detention centers and under state supervision are less dangerous to the world around them than the world is to them" (Richie, 2005, p. 76). African American girls do not commit more crimes than other girls. However, they typically do not have resources for an attorney other than a public defender, and they will more than likely serve all their time, as few are able to meet bail requirements. When families are already struggling, transportation to a facility that is out of town is often unobtainable. Without visits and support, girls are further isolated and left to make more decisions on their own. Nia experienced this when she was moved about 100 miles outside of the city with no reliable public transportation or rail system between the two cities.

Rewriting the Script

In the context of Girl Time, Black girls are rewriting these scripts. They talk-back and at times acquiesce to institutions of power. However, they use this permissive space to create, question, and imagine something different—a life on their terms as contributors to the world. For the next act I invite stakeholders to the table in order to learn the work that needs to be done.

Magic Carpets and Fairylands
Preparing for a Performance of Possibilities

In the opening scene of "The Switch Around," the characters "Thug Girl" and "Gutta" find themselves in a solitary confinement holding cell. When Gutta asks Thug Girl why she is in solitary confinement, Thug Girl recounts her confrontation with one of the correctional officers. After the characters exchange stories of confrontation and frustration with the detention center personnel, Thug Girl begins to mumble to herself about a legend claiming a magic rug existed somewhere in the prison. According to prison legend, this magical rug could give power over the facility to anyone who stood on it and repeated a series of magical words. Amused, yet curious, Gutta challenges the legend: "I mean I heard about it, but how real is it? To run this joint, that's what's up. But it's only supposed to work in the walls of this prison. It don't change nothing on the outside." Gutta's critique of the legend—that is, that the magic carpet only gave a person power inside the prison walls yet did not wield any influence outside—is at once a mirror and a window to the experiences young people are facing in the school-to-prison pipeline.

This play, written by incarcerated girls in a Girl Time workshop, embodied the politics of desire and yearning in the hearts and minds of girls who—to paraphrase Kaya in Act II—did not "do wrong" as much as they "were wronged." "The Switch Around" was one of the Girl Time plays that blended fantasy and reality. Employing storytelling tropes such as a "magic rug" and old legends, one of the characters, Gutta, raises an important issue. Gutta is not easily impressed by this so-called legend. And why should she be? Gutta wants more than the power to control the facility that imprisons her; she desires power beyond the walls of the prison. Girl Time teaching artists did not solely want girls to have fun while incarcerated; teaching artists wanted girls to know they could create, participate, and have control over their minds even when they were released—to borrow Sanaa's words—into the "open world."

The purpose of this fifth and final act is to raise critical questions about the school-to-prison pipeline, youth justice, and issues impacting girls in order to initiate dialogue and ongoing scholarship and activism that support incarcerated and formerly incarcerated girls as they prepare to reenter schools, communities, and reunite with families. Additionally, I address the ways in which school communities, youth advocates, and scholar-activists are forging paths for incarcerated and formerly incarcerated youth to prepare them for possible lives, as opposed to embracing incarceration discourse. Here I encourage conversations around coalition building and organizing that lure different groups out of their silos and to a table—both metaphorical and real—where ideas and resources can be exchanged and questions can be raised in hopes of finding answers together. Seated at this table will be the girls themselves, parents and guardians, educators and youth advocates, administrators, and scholars. Parents and guardians must be invited to this table. Often in education, parents are blamed when their children do not thrive. In the case of incarcerated and formerly incarcerated children, people assume that a child being jailed is the result of bad parenting; however, it is not always that simple. Many parents are struggling to do the best they can. In spite of the multiple and nuanced stories girls recounted about their home lives, they all wanted their parents to survive and thrive alongside them. Girls wanted resources and support for their families. In this final act, I will first explore the ideology behind creating power sources for girls as opposed to just more programming. I will also push readers to consider the work ahead. Next, I will discuss the power of participation and the ways in which participation and the process of participation can be important in girls' lives. Here I will also share final conversations with two Girl Time student artists, Gabrielle and Jennifer, who returned to Girl Time in spite of having very busy lives and other commitments. Finally, I share lessons learned from both Girl Time student artists and teaching artists drawing from interview data, observed activity, and transcribed dialogue in order to synthesize some of the compelling ideas Girl Time inspires.

Girl Power (Not Just Programs)

At the close of this journey I provide implications for practice, participation, and process in teaching and learning spaces in out-of-school and in-school settings. Typically studies will take winding journeys through various landscapes and end with implications for education narrowly conceptualized as taking place in classrooms. However, my work with Girl Time and other youth-centered projects has taught me that the work is not solely for the schools and classroom teachers alone. Social justice educators work beyond school walls; they are also in community institutions, nonprofit organizations, churches, and recreation centers. There has to be a coalition-building movement addressing the work that needs to be done. Implications for educational research often synthesizes ideas to respond to the question What works? However, research with incarcerated and formerly incarcerated girls as well as their teachers and advocates must begin with a different question—What is the work? (Covington & Bloom, 2003, p. 13). Covington and Bloom further assert, "We need to create a community response to the issues that impact women's lives and increase their risks of incarceration" (p. 13). In creating a community response, we must ask difficult questions that force us to grapple with the work ahead as we contemplate incarcerated and formerly incarcerated girls' lives. I wish to underscore that we are talking about girls in jails; some of the Girl Time student artists first experienced detention at age 13. In our efforts to name the work ahead, I wish to avoid an oversimplistic view of the problem and the solution. For example, Fraden (2001) argues, "The discourse of problem and solution permeates discussions of prison" (p. 120). Enduring questions about incarcerated women plague those who are witnesses to their incarceration as well as advocates of their freedom. Many of these questions also apply to incarcerated girls:

> But what is the problem? Is it personal? (What is *her* problem?) Is it structural? (What is *the* problem?) Is *she* the problem? Is *jail* the problem? Are they both problems and are they both responsible for a solution? (p. 120).

I would further argue that the problem/solution discourse also controls much of education research. To limit a final section, chapter, or, in this case, a final act to implications for education continues to silence the voices of girls and their teachers. It would also undermine the various stakeholders' ability to bring their ideas to the table. There is no single answer just as there is no single story; the narratives of Girl Time teaching artists and student artists demonstrate that there are many factors that contribute to girls' experiencing incarceration and many opportunities that can contribute to their freedom. The first step in this work is to bring everyone to the table.

In my ethnography of student poets in the Bronx, I consider the ways in which the classroom "read and feed" circle, stage, mic, cipher, video camera, and public readings became metaphors for young people to make bold declarations about their current lives, historicized lives, and possible futures (Fisher, 2005a, 2005b, 2007; Winn & Ubiles, in press). Ultimately, the pedagogy leading to a performance of possibilities for these brilliant poets and their teachers, Papa Joe, Amy, and Roland, was about creating a seat at the table even when one had yet to be invited. In the context of Girl Time, the "table" represents a space in which poor youth of color, and girls in particular, can become armed with a sense of worthiness and deservingness. At this table, girls will be able to name their needs—education, critical literacy, opportunities to attend colleges and universities, fruitful careers, safe communities, and access to quality health care for themselves and for their children if they have them. Similarly, Rhodessa Jones' work with incarcerated women challenges the "national seating arrangement" at this so-called table:

> Our national seating arrangement has always been, to put it mildly, tricky, fluid at best. . . . Surveying the individuals who have been deemed unworthy and the reasons why may make us see the shape of the table differently, may make us imagine a taste of something else, may make us survey not only what is but what may be. (Fraden, 2001, p. 132)

While there have been great efforts to create programs that invite girls to sit at the table, Brown (2009) makes a compelling case for why the focus must shift from "programs" to "power":

Even in youth programs aimed at doing things differently by "empower-ing" young people, program processes do not necessarily translate into doing things so that Black girls' and women's voices and bodies are in-cluded, heard, and valued. Therefore, when Black girls act up, they are often made out to be the problem rather than the program [being the problem]. But Black girls are not the problem. Neither is their often-called disruptive behavior. What their actions embody are types of knowledge about the ways the world works for Black girls living, working, and/or studying in a particular time and space. These types of knowledge are too often punished and disciplined rather than seen as partial answers to the messy yet critical questions, such as Black girl celebration—for what purpose? And for whom? In many cases, their actions question program-ming: And to whose benefit? Empowerment for whose sake? (p. 27)

Brown's response to the needs of Black girls manifested in SOLHOT or Saving Our Lives, Hear Our Truths!. In the context of SOLHOT, Brown and her fellow participants privilege the stories of Black girls and women. In an effort to move beyond mentoring programs that can recreate hier-archical relationships, girls and women in SOLHOT interrogate "popular messages and stereotypes about Black girls" together. And in this circle of what Brown refers to as Black girlhood celebration, the boundaries of mentor/mentee; expert/novice; teacher/student are blurred or, as Brown asserts, "We think of ourselves as both narrator and the audience, actively resisting narratives of Black girlhood that do not include us" (p. 24).

While his work does not focus solely on Black girls, Ginwright's (2010) call for "radical healing" is key to the work that needs to be done with in-carcerated and formerly incarcerated girls. Radical healing, according to Ginwright, includes four key elements: caring relationships, community, critical consciousness, and culture:

Healing occurs in everyday life when black youth confront racial pro-filing in their neighborhoods, fight for free bus passes to get to school, demand access to bathrooms that work in their schools, and present im-promptu theatre on street corners to inspire youth to vote. These acts require a consciousness of possibilities and are fostered through strong, caring relationships and spaces that encourage black youth to see beyond present day community conditions. When black youth are conscious of the root causes of the problems they face, they act in profound ways to resist and transform issues they view as unjust. (p. 8)

Similar to Brown's work with SOLHOT, Ginwright co-created a camp for Black youth with one of his former students; this camp planted the seeds that foster participation and activism. This is one of the long-term goals of Girl Time; teaching artists would like to create a pipeline of possibilities through which Girl Time alumni can return to the program as teachers and share their wisdom, insight, and creativity with new ensembles of girls. Girl Time's goal to create a pipeline of possibilities began with the after-school program for upper elementary and middle school girls who had not experienced the juvenile justice system. The after-school program, which first began in a city recreation center, grew to include a public middle school located in the heart of the city serving African American students. Girl Time's effort to maintain this pipeline was further cultivated in a public event inviting various stakeholders to share and exchange resources that girls needed. These projects are currently being further developed.

Planting the Seeds of Participation

One of the first questions people often ask me about Girl Time is how many of the girls stay out of detention centers, jails, prisons, or "trouble" as a result of this program. This question is flawed and any response I could attempt to provide would be equally as flawed. For even when girls stay "out of trouble," I cannot empirically support their recidivism as a result of the program. Nor could I say Girl Time failed if a girl returns to a detention center. A 2-day Girl Time workshop in an RYDC or the Girl Time summer program does not and cannot undo the years of miseducation and dispossession many girls' experience. In her preface to *Imagining Medea: Rhodessa Jones and Theater for Incarcerated Women*, Angela Y. Davis (2001) observes, "While the rehearsals and performances may indeed create momentary transcendences, imprisonment continues to define the women's everyday realities where their social and psychic problems continue to play themselves out" (Davis in Fraden, 2001, p. x). Indeed the "momentary transcendences" give all of us—teaching artists, student artists, audience members, families—a sense of hope, great pride, and the gift of witnessing the best in each other with the knowledge there is more to come. However, it is participation and the process of participation that is central to working with girls:

Everything starts with participation. What the participation comes to mean in the life of a person may not be known now or ever be knowable, but one should not therefore infer that participation has not made a difference. . . . Participation opens up more possibilities for exchange, different combinatory ways to make community; it may enable change, though it can't ensure it. (Fraden, 2001, p. xv)

During the Girl Time summer 2010 program, I continued as a teaching artist, or the Girl Time "historian," as Kaya began to refer to me (Fisher, 2008). Now a summer tradition, I could not imagine missing the summer program and the opportunity to reunite with returning teaching and student artists as well as meet new members of the ensemble. When I walked in the multi-service center, I saw a familiar face. I quickly realized I was looking at Gabrielle, who was a student artist in the summer 2007 program. Gabrielle did not return to the summer program in 2008 or 2009; however, there she was smiling broadly and running towards me. I could never forget Gabrielle; she was always impeccably and creatively dressed with accessories galore. Gabrielle and her boyfriend, Zeus, were the proud parents of a baby girl and Zeus would often wait in the multi-service center for Gabrielle for sometimes as many as four or five hours while she rehearsed during that first summer that we met. During that first summer I remember Gabrielle correcting me when I referred to Zeus as her "boyfriend." Gabrielle insisted he was her "baby daddy" because she believed that was a step higher than a "boyfriend." Of course, Gabrielle's daughter was always decked out from head to toe, just like her mother, wearing brightly hued sun dresses with plenty of bows and hair decor to match. I also could not forget Gabrielle from her stunning performance as Ashley in "Ride or Die" (see Act IV) as well as one of the talking wigs in "Hair Drama." Gabrielle updated me on her life: She was 19 years old and she and Zeus (who she now referred to as her "boyfriend" and "the father of my children") were now the proud parents of three children. Gabrielle had completed a medical assistant program and was doing in-home health care for clients. Her dream was to become a physician's assistant but she had no clue what path to take. When I told her my best friend was a physician's assistant and I could put them in touch she squealed with delight. We agreed that it would be a great idea to sit down together during some downtime and catch up. I was beyond curious as to why this young woman would show up at the multi-service center seeking a connection with girls and women even as she led a busy life as a mother, partner, and health care provider:

Well really I was thinking the other day—I still have that picture that I took in 2007—[and] I was looking at that picture and thinking to myself, "I don't really look the same." I guess because I was younger and my whole mentality was younger and childish. I was saying to myself, "I've really grown." I was thinking I would like to come back today and see how the young ladies [are] in the program today.

Referring to the headshots as well as the candid photos that we took throughout the summer program and presented to the girls after their final performance, Gabrielle could see her personal growth and development. She hoped that she could witness the growth and development of other girls as well:

> Even though I'm still young I talk like I am so much older. But even though I've matured I want to be around the young girls in there. I see myself in all them. The way they act, their body movement, I really see myself in all of 'em. I really want to tell my story because I've been through a lot when I was younger. Throughout the years I have really matured and changed in many ways.

To hear Gabrielle discuss the ways in which she could see herself in the other girls further supported the long-term goals of Girl Time; former student artists still needed and wanted to be a part of an ensemble and had so much to offer by way of working side by side with girls who shared many experiences and whose lives also contrasted. Gabrielle marveled over her own mindset when she began the Girl Time process and how much she could not understand some of the decisions she made in the past:

> I think it was basically like peer pressure. The things I used to do I thought [were] right. I had a mindset that thought running away was good [and] skipping school was good. I actually thought that! But now when I look back there is so much stuff that I did that I look back on. . . . I don't regret it because I think if I hadn't done those things I wouldn't have known what it felt like to do things like that. When I look back on things like that, I just don't understand how I could do things like that. Because in my mind I really thought those things was right. Running [away] was cool. I was lying telling people my mother was dead. My mother means a lot to me now. I was just doing so [many]

childish things and I just don't know how I could let myself do things such as that. But I think it was peer pressure like during that time I had to move back with my mother. . . . She a good grandmother now to my kids but with us she wasn't too good. I don't want to blame her because I did have my own mind. I just didn't get the guidance that I needed from her.

Gabrielle's self-reflection was a powerful testimony that children and youth often view the world from a different vantage point than adults. At 19 she already felt wiser than the 16-year-old girl I first met. Again, Gabrielle did not wish to blame her mother, although she wished her mother had provided more guidance. Gabrielle was determined to be the mother she did not have and took pride in the fact that she and Zeus were figuring out how to be supportive parents together. Gabrielle also did not wish to blame her school. "There were counselors," explained Gabrielle, "but it was up to the kids to want to work with the counselors." Gabrielle believed that you had to be proactive to get what you wanted out of high school and that was not something she was able to do at the time. She felt distracted by other things in life including what her peers were doing, how to obtain material possessions, creating a healthy relationship with her mother, and seeking companionship. While she was only 19, Gabrielle felt worlds away from her earlier teen years and especially when she was 13 and first found herself in Main RYDC:

Yeah, I was [in Main RYDC] for 6 months. Those were my younger days. But I mean it makes me feel good how God can take me out of one situation and bring me into another situation. Like our stories that we be creating brings a lot out. A lot of the stories that we write that the girls are acting out [are] real life. I know a lot of the girls locked up in the detention center have been in [those] situations. So it feels good to let them know that they are able to express their feelings because every female, everybody goes through stuff. So I guess we bring the character out in them.

Gabrielle asked me a series of questions. She wanted to know how long I went to school, how I stayed motivated, what I was currently doing and how I liked it. "You just have everything put together," Gabrielle declared after hearing my responses. I remembered my conversation with Zaire about appearing perfect and wanted to make my own process more transparent. "You know, it's always in progress," I explained, "I always want to do better. What I do is never enough." Gabrielle kept asking questions, "Can I ask about your baby?" she asked (I was about 4 months pregnant when we sat down together). She wanted to know how far along I was, how many children I wanted, and if I had morning sickness. When I put Gabrielle in touch with my best friend who was a physician's assistant, the career Gabrielle wanted more than anything, she had more questions, such as how long the program took and what she had to do to prepare. My best friend and I kept using the abbreviated term *pre-reqs*, and Gabrielle stopped to ask, "What's a pre-req?" Gabrielle's honest questions reminded me of how comfortable we had become with our jargon and nicknames in the academy and throughout our schooling experiences that we could isolate others without even realizing it. I was excited that Gabrielle felt comfortable enough to ask questions and did not want anything to get in the way of her learning. She gave me a new perspective on the ways in which formerly incarcerated girls need to be invited to the table.

During the 2010 summer program I also had the opportunity to spend time with Jennifer who was a summer 2009 participant. When I met Jennifer in the summer 2009 she was on her way to college in the fall. Jennifer's experiences were vastly different from Gabrielle's experiences. Gabrielle yearned to be in college and live in the dorms, but having three children removed dorm life from her options. Jennifer just completed her first year in college as a biology major and recently learned that she could have two majors. "I'm going to do child care as well . . . those are my two passions. I love children and I love science," explained Jennifer. While Gabrielle and Jennifer's lives contrast, I use their experiences here to underscore the importance of the process of participation and ongoing participation. Jennifer wanted to return to Girl Time to reconnect with the "overwhelming feeling" she had at the theatre where the public performance took place:

> When we first came into the theatre you see all of our pictures. We are performing to an audience. There may be one hundred, two hundred people, maybe more. It was just like we all got a standing ovation. First I thought it was a simple play. I thought we were just going to be doing regular plays and not a lot of people would come. But, it turned out to be something really important—it surprised me and that's what makes me do it.

Jennifer did not believe that so many people would be interested in her story and the stories of her peers until she saw the standing room only crowd in the public theatre. That surprise and joy of being recognized was something that she wanted to return to even as she embarked on her new life as a university student. Jennifer's family—a close-knit foster care home for girls—was a big part of her network. When she discussed overcoming her first semester struggles such as time management, she revealed that she did not overcome her obstacles alone:

> My family is not my biological family, because I live in a group home. From staff members to case managers—and I have a mentor—so they really helped me out a lot. . . . I'm still in the group home—a lot of us are—so that I will have somewhere to stay when I come home from college. It's a Christian organization. I think they work there because they enjoy it and it's not just a job. They treat us like family members not just like another child that they have on their caseload.

In Act IV, I briefly discuss the ways in which many foster children find themselves entangled in the school-to-prison pipeline. Jennifer was in a very supportive environment, and her story confirmed how important it was for formerly incarcerated girls to have multiple resources, multiple mentors and various types of support. Jennifer was also able to rebuild with her mother. "What helped me was sitting and talking to [my mother]. She really motivated me to do a lot. She explained she didn't want me to be like her . . . that's been my biggest motivation," explained Jennifer. As one of the 1.5 million children of incarcerated parents, Jennifer was able to go to her mother for wisdom and advice. Being able to see her mother along with the guidance of her mentors and counselors prepared Jennifer for college:

> A lot of people are afraid to talk to counselors because they don't want them in their business. But it actually helps out to tell someone what you have on your chest. I feel like getting over a situation is to talk about the situation. . . . When I was in high school I just felt like I really didn't want to do anything. I felt like it was worthless. I was getting bad grades. Everything I did would turn into something bad so I just quit. . . . What really brought me to reality was that if I got kicked out of my group home, where was I going? Then it brought me back to what my mother told me that I keep going down that road then I am going to end up just like she did. So, I just really had to change.

Participating in Girl Time was an extension of the network of support that Jennifer had and a way she could continue to explore the possibilities of her life beyond incarceration and beyond foster care. After our experiences with Jada, Kaya decided to be more flexible with returning student artists and not limit the age to 18. Jennifer still needed Girl Time just like she needed her mother's wisdom and the support of her foster family. Jennifer, like many of her Girl Time peers, felt like her performance—especially in the detention centers—showed that although she was "one of them," that "it doesn't always have to be like that":

I think performing makes me feel that I have risen above my circumstances. I am not the person I was when I was younger. Performing makes me feel really good about myself. It makes me feel like I am not another foster care statistic because a lot of us do get arrested for being runaways and end up in detention facilities. Performing makes me feel like I rose above my situation. And at the time when I was in the [detention center] audience I used to wish I was one of the actors who could perform and walk out the front door. It feels great to actually do it.

While participation and the process of participation were central to Girl Time, there were many other lessons from both student artists and teaching artists. In the final sections I seek to address what the girls and women in this ensemble taught me.

Learning from Student Artists

Writing. Participants in Girl Time were writing; they were writing before they went into detention centers and prior to being asked to write a play. While playwriting was, in most cases, a new form of writing for the girls I interviewed, they found it to be a surprising extension of the kinds of writing they were already doing. Girls wrote poetry, songs, journal entries, and one girl in particular, Rae, was working on her autobiography. Rae, one of the voices in the introduction of this book, participated in the summer 2008 program. Rae was part of a collective of four girls who participated that summer who lived in a foster home together. When I interviewed Rae, she came with stacks of journals and loose papers that were worn and tattered:

Maisha: Do you do any kinds of writing? Have you ever written a play before?

Rae: No, I'm writing a book now. But ya'll kinda interrupted. I
    can't write this whole week.

Maisha: We interrupted?

Rae: Yea.

Maisha: What is this? Is this a journal that you're keeping?

Rae: No, I'm writing a book.

Maisha: About what?

Rae: It's about me. My life.

Maisha: An autobiography?

Rae: Yea.

Maisha: So where does it begin?

Rae: I started it when I was younger. I had a house fire and the
    fire started it was my sister's birthday. I forget which one.
    We was poor so we was all in the closet and my brother
    had some change so he went to the store and bought a 25
    cent cake. We had a candle and we was all singing happy
    birthday in a little bitty closet and we were gonna give my
    sister her present. So my sister had the candle and she got
    scared and dropped it. She dropped it on the bike tire. As it
    got bigger, she got scared and pushed me in the fire and ran
    out and shut me in the closet. And my brother came back to
    get me. (Interview, June 2008)

Rae voluntarily brought her writing to me when we discussed sitting down for an interview. She had also shared her journal with Kaya and some of her ensemble members. In my work with spoken-word poetry, open-mic communities, I learned that many poets and writers were closeted writers throughout their youth. These men and women kept journals, folded pieces of papers, or sometimes committed to memory poetry, prose, songs, and raps (Fisher, 2003, 2004, 2007, 2009). Many poets reported that they never excelled in English or Language Arts classes and it was not until they participated in spoken-word poetry, open-mic events, Black bookstore readings, or what I refer to as participatory literacy communities (PLCs) in out-of-school contexts that they began to cultivate their writing through peer networks, workshops, and performing their writing. Sanaa saw a link between her writing and her grandmother's acknowledgment that she was "doing something positive." For Sanaa, the ability to write or view oneself as a writer was inextricably linked to her humanity. Writing was also the place where formerly incarcerated girls could confront anger, disappointment, and fear as well as anticipate next steps. Sanaa also viewed writing as a form of power, through which she could have more control over her actions because she worked through issues while writing. Tichina, another voice in the prelude to this book, was journaling before Girl Time. When Tichina shared with me that she had interest in science and fire—she served 1 year in detention after setting fire to a deserted building near her apartment complex—it was her journal that helped her check in with herself daily:

> *Maisha*: Share something with us that makes you very proud of yourself. What are you most proud of that we may not know about that you'd like to share?
>
> *Tichina*: I'm talented and I got my own style . . . I write in my journal, that's it.
>
> *Maisha*: Is this a journal for school or for you?
>
> *Tichina*: For me, for my feelings. I write whatever happens that day. Whether I'm having a good day or a bad day.
>
> *Maisha*: Do you keep it in a binder? Or is it actually like a little journal?
>
> *Tichina*: It's a composition book . . . Sometimes I let people read it, but it's my feelings and stuff.

Tichina's journal became even more sacred to her after the arson incident; she was able to use it throughout her counseling and to help her communicate with her family.

Performing. For girls who have been inundated with labels—troubled, delinquent, bad, promiscuous, and others—performing was a way for them to reintroduce themselves to the world on their own terms. Nia described her performances as "proving" herself to others and "making a story" out of people who condemned her. Lisa took the DVD I made for the girls of their summer 2007 performance to the judge who resided over her pending probation; the judge was so pleased about her participation and performance that he approved ending her probation period and encouraged her to continue her work in theatre. Participation was viewed as something constructive and helped many girls demonstrate their worthiness. What I learned was that the girls I interviewed were ready to move past their incarceration experiences; they were waiting for the people around them who could not find a way to forgive them or to see them beyond the mistakes that led to their detention in the first place. Performing showed families, Department of Juvenile Justice employees, and the public what the girls had already begun to believe about themselves: they were capable and motivated to be a part of something meaningful.

Ensemble Building. While all of the themes are important; the notion of girls using the Girl Time community to learn how to build ensemble with other girls and women was, perhaps, one of the most compelling. Girls had learned to loathe the company of other girls before their incarceration (which was only exacerbated in detention); they embraced an ideology that females were not to be trusted and could never want the best for you. Dismantling this deep-seated belief was hard work but something that theatre does well. Jennifer said that working with an ensemble in Girl Time helped her prepare for dorm life in college:

> The number one thing I learned in Girl Time was to deal with women—other women. To respect their space and respect them as a whole. At school, dorm-wise, I share with a lot of different women, a lot of different ages, a lot of different attitudes coming from so many different places and it's the same with Girl Time. A lot of us have our own problems and issues but when it comes to the plays you set all that aside to finish a goal. Same with school. You set that stuff to the side to finish school.

Trust, I learned, is at the core of theatre; every person involved in theatre is dependent on someone else and no one person is more important than another person. The audience has value equal to the actors, the director, the stage manager, the lighting director, the sound engineer, and so on. As both Kaya and Zaire explained to the girls before the set foot in the theater, it was not about anyone individually, and everyone had to come ready to work toward the same goal:

> Remember, when we get to the theatre it's not about us. It's about telling the story, so we have to put everything together— the story, the performance, the costumes, and the lights, sounds, and everything. (Kaya, field notes, June 21, 2007)

Zaire reminded girls the day before the performance:

> Remember, when you come in tomorrow it's not about you. It's about the entire community, the audience. Leave the attitudes at the door. (Zaire, field notes, June 22, 2007)

Creating a Discourse of Second Chances. Girl Time provided a neutral space that welcomed girls where they stood, as opposed to continuing to make them feel ashamed about where they had been. There was no finger wagging about teenage pregnancy; many of the girls were mothers and it was pointless to continuously punish them for this fact. The safety net that Girl Time created for girls and for women was what brought girls back to the circle. Gabrielle and Jennifer knew they had their Girl Time "home" to return to when they needed to renew their sense of participation and ensemble.

Youth Advocacy. One of the strengths of being able to interview girls multiple times was that I was able to follow their lives as they journeyed through various life stages and institutions. I found that girls needed advocates to help them navigate institutions, especially schools, as they returned from detention. Nia, Lisa, and Janelle had no idea where to begin after missing school during their incarceration. Nia was taking classes at a continuation high school from which the history teacher was absent for weeks, and students were unsure if they would be ready for the graduation test since the substitute did not have a history background. Lisa did not know what questions to ask about returning to school and could not figure out if she should take the GED or try to finish at a continuation school. Janelle had moved around so much and missed so much school that she needed someone to sit down, look at her transcripts, and create a plan of action. There were other resources that girls sorely needed and one of the most important was an attorney. When my friend who recently finished law school came to see one of the Girl Time RYDC workshops, she found herself surrounded by girls when they learned she recently completed her law degree. Their questions ranged from very complicated issues around their specific cases to more basic questions that demonstrated how little they knew about what they were facing. Parents needed advocates for their children as well. For example, parents would often talk to teaching artists about issues that schools and other institutions needed to know about; however, they did not always feel safe or welcome to speak to people they deemed to be authority figures. My experiences with Girl Time parents informed my work with grade-level teams at a public high school where I served as an instructional coach. When grade-level teams met with parents I tried to support them by encouraging language that indicated that teachers and parents would work together, as opposed to teachers giving parents a laundry list of the students' problems and their concerns.

Talking Back. Talk-backs that followed performances were powerful. In the context of the talk-backs, plays written by incarcerated girls served as mediating tools for young people to discuss issues that were relevant to their lives. Talk-backs in the RYDCs—like the one that opened Act III—were perhaps, the most compelling because of the opportunity for formerly incarcerated and currently incarcerated youth to address issues and topics that impacted their lives. In summer 2008, Girl Time was able to perform in two RYDCs; what was interesting about these two performances was that both audiences consisted mostly of boys, which made Girl Time student artists extremely nervous and self-conscious. At one point, Kaya and I stood behind the audience and had to act as cheerleaders—jumping, smiling, encouraging—as we saw the power and the energy of the girls being sucked away by the presence of so many boys. This scene reminded me of Rhodessa Jones' work with incarcerated women; she explained that when men were around the entire theatre workshop would practically crumble. Jones attempted to facilitate coed theatre workshops but she could not get the women to focus. However, in both cases when we had the largely male audience, it was the talk-back that saved the day. When we got to Stallworth RYDC, Kaya gave a shout out to one of our playwrights who was in the audience and who participated in our last workshop at that location. "It just shows you can write a story and have it brought to life!" declared Kaya. The girl just beamed as everyone turned to look and cheer for her. Kaya continued with the audience, "Did you like the plays? Which ones?"

> *Boy*: All of them.
> *Girl*: "Life of Teen Parents" when the father went to get the child.
> *Boy*: The play about the cat and dog—it was funny.
> *Boy*: I liked the play about teen parents—it showed us we need
>   to be more responsible.

All the girls did an unrehearsed yet collective "Awwww!" Teaching artists smiled and shook their heads. One boy turned the talk-back around and asked student artists which plays were their favorites:

> *Lisa*: "Cats and Dogs" because we are like cats and dogs, you
>   know, we are in the same house like brothers and sisters
>   about to fight.
> *Student artist*: "The Big Leave" because you have to have hope
>   and also "The Witch and the Boy" because the boy was

smart and I'm trying to teach my brother to beware of
strangers.

Boy: Why do y'all do this?

Student artist: We do this to encourage y'all to do something
better.

Sanaa: I used to be bad and I changed and hope to change other
girls before they get in danger.

Boy: I liked the [play] with the abusive boyfriend. Shawty
(referring to Julisa's stunning performance as an abusive
boyfriend) did that right especially her body language and
her eyes.

Julisa stood up in character and gave a stare, much to everyone's
delight.

Lisa: I just have one thing to say to y'all. I have a son and his
father doesn't do nothing for him so I'm like a mother and a
father. I hope if you have kids you take care of them and do
for them.

First there was a pause and then everyone clapped for Lisa. Suddenly, one of the boys raised his hand and shared that he wrote a book and that he writes poetry. He volunteered to share his poem. "Y'all ready?" I think all of us were still stunned and, of course, delighted that this young man offered to share his work. "My life, my glory, my story . . . " went the beginning of his piece. Not only did he recite his poem from memory but it was rich in melody and cadence. When our poet/hero finished everyone screamed, stood up, and cheered (and a few of the teaching artists fought tears). It felt like a triumphant moment and we all were left to wonder why these talented children were locked away from the world. The newly crowned poet/hero responded, "Thank you—I enjoyed the plays."

We arrived at Meadow RYDC later that afternoon—the institution that Sanaa claimed had "soft bread" and where the JCOs were "like mothers." I did not get to see any soft bread and after hearing one of the JCOs yell at some of the boys I was not so sure what to make of the comparison to mothers, either. When I conducted the "house count," again, it was mostly boys—26 were Black and 10 were White—with 7 eerily silent Black girls. There was an army of guards along the periphery—all Black—who were looking very serious. Kaya and I stood in the back behind the boys doing our cheerleader thing again hoping to keep the student artists focused. After the performance—which went really well—Anne led the talk-back:

Anne: What plays did you like?
Boy: I liked the one with teen parents.

There was silence and wait time; no one was really raising their hand or participating in this talk-back. I began to imagine how much fun Zaire would have had with this group. Finally, one of the Black boys broke the silence with an unexpected question:

Boy: Is this organization a nonprofit?
Anne: Yes, how do you know this?
Boy: I've read about nonprofits and also seen some things on
    television about them.

Anne seemed taken off guard by this question but used the last performance as an opportunity to identify any writers who may have been in the audience:

Anne: Do any of you write?

Many answered, "Yes," at once and then pointed out the inmates who they knew were writers, rappers, and poets. It was inspiring to see how the writers were already known among their peer group. Another Black boy asked a question:

Boy: How many of y'all been locked up?

When all of our girls raised their hands except Tempest, the boys looked at each other incredulously.

Boy: Y'all don't look like you fit in here.

The girls laughed and even a few guards had to give in as well. Lisa turned the questioning around to the boys:

Lisa: How many of y'all have children?

So many hands went up that I could not count. It seemed as if every boy—Black and White—raised their hand as did a few of the girls. Lisa decided that these talk-backs were her opportunities to raise issues about single teenage parenting and the roles of the teen fathers:

Lisa: Let me tell y'all something. I have a son and his daddy is
    locked up. Y'all need to take care of your children. I have to
    do everything by myself!

The girls started cheering and then a few boys gave in and applauded
Lisa's bold declaration. It was as if the teaching artists and guards had
completely disappeared and the youth were working things out on their
own.

Janet: I have something for y'all. I am going to share a rap I wrote
    when I was locked up and I am going to challenge one of
    you to share one but it has to be positive and about how
    your future is going to be. Anyone want to challenge it?

Janet, one of the student artists, launched into a rap about what she
used to do and how she once ran the streets in a rage of violence. When
she finished everyone cheered. Kaya and I exchanged looks of disbelief;
we had no idea she could rap. Suddenly, a lanky White boy stood up in
front of his seat until his peers shouted for him to go in front of the audience onto our makeshift stage. He started to rap without hesitation, "My
only friends are metaphors and similes . . . " he began and the crowd
went wild. When he was finished everyone was shouting, cheering, and
a few even compared him to the rapper "Eminem." On his way back to
his seat—he was the only White boy who sat among the Black boys, while
the other White boys all sat together—he received plenty of fist bumps
and high fives.

During our downtime the girls expressed how overwhelmed they
were by the opportunity to have an exchange with incarcerated youth.
The adults stepped back and the youth talked. Girls (and teachers)
were excited that something they created and brought to life inspired
other writers. I would have given anything to be able to interview the
audience members at the detention centers to hear more about how
they viewed the girls' performance, but the impromptu cipher spoke
volumes.

Learning from Teaching Artists

Relationships vs. Roles. Girl Time teaching artists privileged relationships over roles. In other words, teaching artists were not consumed by
their titles as teachers but were more interested in developing a relation-

ship with each girl. Girls used our first names, however, they would often choose to put a "Ms." in the front of our first names, which was a sign of respect. This respect was earned rather than demanded. Building, nurturing, and maintaining these relationships during official teaching time or what Ginger referred to as "downtime" were also key to fostering relationships.

Ensemble as a Metaphor for a Learning Community. Girl Time teaching artists lived by ensemble. Petulia had a vision of ensemble that encapsulated the work that needs to be done with youth, and with girls in particular:

> Ensemble creates safety. If you know these people are on your side, you are gonna feel more comfortable taking risks. We all thrive in a community of people that care about us. Maybe not all of us, but you know you are much more likely to thrive and blossom and explore and take risks when you trust the people with whom you can be present. (Interview, 2007)

Creating safety was a priority and I would argue safety is important for both student artists and teaching artists. Teaching artists created ensemble in pre-meetings and during teacher training so they could be ready to create ensemble with student artists. Isis also had a vision of ensemble that focused specifically on group dynamics:

> I think the ensemble building is also important because it deals with the power dynamics within the group, which is very apparent because incarcerated girls are in this insular unit, being locked up together, and so those power dynamics spiral exponentially. So when we come in from the outside we see almost immediately, "Okay this girl is in control. She holds the energy of the room, whatever she does, people follow." And I think the ensemble building diminishes some of that but it also collides with community in a way that we don't necessarily confront it openly, but we may pull one of the young ladies to the side and say, "You know, you're a leader in this group so we need you to step up and be a leader in what we are doing." So in that way it does sort of help those who do have that leadership by cultivating [leadership] in a positive way, where they're not just leading for their own motives, but leading for the good of the group. (Interview, 2007)

Building ensemble also demonstrated the power of team teaching; when teachers work together students have a rich opportunity to experience multiple ways of thinking, communicating, and decisionmaking. If the classroom could be reimagined as an ensemble—including teachers and students—working to reach the same goals, there could be a new way for teachers and students to connect. They could move with each other, establish a rhythm, and begin to learn to trust.

Common Denominators. All of the teaching artists saw their lives converging with formerly incarcerated girls by virtue of being women who had stood in their place—adolescence, yearning for companionship, and the opportunity to be chosen by somebody—once before. For Kaya and Anne, they saw their lives converge with the girls through what Kaya referred to as "the desire for love." Some of the teaching artists may not have shared the exact same lived experiences as the girls; however, they all agreed that the desire of love, feeling rejected by love, and being rendered voiceless by men (and women) were universal experiences.

Recovery on the Road. During one of my first Girl Time workshops in an RYDC, we were interrupted by an emergency count. All of us were escorted to the parking lot and proceeded to wait outside for what seemed an eternity. Girls were in the middle of finishing their plays and we were doubtful we could get the ensemble reignited knowing girls would have to endure a strip search and other forms of humiliation before the count was all over. However, when we returned the girls were indeed disoriented but also hungry to do the work. Kaya explained to the girls that in theatre their response to an unexpected interruption was referred to as "recovery on the road." The beauty of recovery on the road was that even in the midst of chaos it was still possible to recover and move toward the goals of the ensemble.

Committing. Throughout my observations of Girl Time, teaching artists used the term *commit* with the girls as they prepared for their performance of possibilities. While this one word seems so simple, it has important implications when working with girls. Mindy defined *committing* in the context of her role as a Girl Time teaching artist:

> When I talk about committing as a theatre artist, I mean owning whatever that character is . . . truly owning that character with the full amount of energy involved with that and the full amount

of intensity involved. Oftentimes you say the word *energy* to people and they think you have to move a lot. And I guess it's not so much energy but intensity that you're asking for. To commit vocally, means that you're going to use different levels. I'm not going to say, "I'm angry and this is what angry looks like." You need to explore. When you commit as an actor, as a performer, it means that you're committing to an exploration, to discovering the best way in which to interpret something and to do so in such a way that your final product is something that feels true to you. . . . It means that you keep exploring and that there is constant exploration and that there isn't a final product. . . . The commitment to the process and with the girls especially [is] committing not only to your character but committing to the support of your entire ensemble. And as a [teaching artist], you're committing to supporting the entire ensemble, which means not saying, "That was wrong, you need to do it this way, this is how you fix that"—[but] learning how to support each other in each person's individual process and committing to each other just in terms of committing to be here, to participate, to give you my energy when I am here. I commit to give you my focus, my concentration. (Interview, 2007)

Some Final Thoughts

In the prologue to this manuscript, written in five acts, I challenged readers to reject the single story of incarcerated and formerly incarcerated girls as dangerous, unworthy, and undeserving of an audience. Children in detention centers, jails, and prisons are not an indication that something is wrong with our youth. Incarcerated children should be a signal to adults that there is work to do and that youth need opportunities to be heard. While I have introduced the voices of girls who experienced incarceration and educators who seek to foster their sense of creativity, independence, and value, I know that simply asking readers to hear these voices is not enough:

> The performance of possibility does not arrogantly assume that we exclusively are giving voice to the silenced, for we understand that they speak and have been speaking in places often foreign to us. Nor are we assuming that we possess the unequivocal knowledge and skills to enable people to intervene in injustice—or that they have not been intervening through various other forms all the time. (Madison, 2005, p. 178)

A community response to the incarceration of girls must move beyond "the acknowledgement of voice" to "actual engagement" (p. 173–174). The narratives of Girl Time teaching artists, as well as the lived experiences of formerly incarcerated girls throughout these acts are tools for discussion, analysis, and critique. They can and should be used in families, community organizations, schools, and any institutions committed to serving youth, and Black girls in particular. I invite and encourage readers to "talk-back" to this text and the texts embedded within, for in this performance, the audience as well as the performers are left with enduring questions about what the next act(s) will be as they are both in the process of becoming.

Talk-Back/Talk-With

How Does One Applaud in Text?

Michelle Fine

"Girl Time brings me out into a whole different environment. It's like I'm under a whole new sky or something." (Jada)

"Theatre is a weapon of liberation." (Boal, 1979)

"I am a seed planter." (Zaire)

With the stunning insights of Jada, Zaire, Boal, and other great thinkers, *Girl Time* is a rich, hopeful, and provocative performance of life in the subjunctive; life as it is and as it might be for young women entangled in the juvenile justice system, and slightly older women lucky enough to be entangled with these young women.

In the brilliant hands of Maisha T. Winn, *Girl Time* harvests seeds and stories about girls living in juvenile settings, refusing the dominant script of bad/promiscuous/damaged and resisting the equally problematic romance with victim/innocent/redemptive heroine. From prologue to finale, the story unfolds, guided by the caution, "Show a people as only one thing ... and that is what they become" (Adichie, 2009). Winn is driven by the conviction that the single story "robs people of humanity." Instead she serves up a feast of stories, a bouillabaisse of affect, a performative canvas for painting a new sky, cultivating new seeds—all elements, perhaps, in a movement for young women's liberation.

Penned in the ink of love, awe, despair, and dignity, the volume swings between documentary and possibility. *Girl Time* documents the circuits of dispossession that choke off opportunity in the lives of the girls and, at

145

the same time, captures the visions young women have for themselves and their babies—the imagination for "what could be" cultivated by the teaching artists in respectful conversation and intimacy with the young women artists.

> "Your name is something that no one can ever take away from you. Sometimes we don't like our names but we have to claim them and say them in a way that people know how we feel about ourselves. I know you can do it. Show us what you got."
> (Zaire)

A blend of ethnography and participant observation, a study of lives and engaged action research, the volume offers a sensual journey of re-vision as enfleshed and enacted by the ensemble of young women and teaching artists. There is the deliberate grounding of the work in the sights, smells, touch, tastes, and affects of the young women; the sweat and struggle of the theatre group; the gifts and ambivalence of the teach-ing artists; the steely smells of barbed wire and metal detectors. And yet lifting off the page an ironic sensibility floats that something else is pos-sible, "under a whole new sky," even in the difficult confines of human containment.

It is this twisted irony of devastation and dreams that captivates a reader, narrated by a gifted writer, acted by talented teachers and stu-dents, in a setting of confinement where sometimes "the bread is soft" and "JCOs are just like mommies." Winn does not try to deliver a narrative of coherence. The braiding of silencing and voice within State facilities pierces like a splinter on the soul of the audience, insisting that we attend to the contradictions and scratches that penetrate the bodies and minds of young women growing up in neoliberal, overincarcerating America.

With deep appreciation to Maisha Winn, the young women, the art-ists, and Winn's parents who "saved me by pumping Black Nationalism into my veins," I craft my Talk-Back to muse about two words that mature and metabolize across the chapters: *freedom* and *commitment*.

Freedom

Winn's manuscript arrived at my home a day after I returned from teach-ing at a university in Turkey. As I wandered through the Topkapi Palace (1465–1856) and the internal quarters for the Harem in Istanbul, I listened carefully and incredulously as the tour guide told us, "This was really a university, not what you think." I thought of the young women, "beauties and intelligent," taken from families to "serve" the sultan and the "dark skinned eunuchs" who watched over them to protect them. Stunned that the institution was being framed as a university, I asked if the "concubines" ever got pregnant, and, indeed, "Yes, they did. The sultan's children were permitted to kill the children of concubines but not with knives, only rope. It was not a crime to kill the children; it was a crime to spill royal blood." You do the math of rape, sexual abuse of women called concubines and men called eunuchs, the tragic intersections of gender, race, class, and sexuality colonized for power.

Who gets to tell the story and whose subjectivities are smothered?

Maisha Winn delivers us a very embodied, contradictory, and participatory story of freedom within confined places.

Refusing the simplicity of a simple narrative (either university or sex trafficking in the case of the Harem), Winn holds the hands and hearts of readers as we enter depressing spaces of confinement and listen to the passions and terrors of the young women. Winn insists that we contend with the question: Where do girls and young women find freedom and voice *in and out of* juvenile residences and foster care, urban schools and public housing—maybe even in the harem?

By way of answer she escorts us into Our Place, where young women in State facilities are invited to speak, perform, dramatize, and talk-back. Both inside and out, many of these young women have been systematically denied human rights and freedom—the capacity and opportunity to act on a whim, to speak one's mind, to breathe with comfort, to relax in a space of human security, to be scared and held, to be educated, to be heard, to be free of violence. To make a mistake. To the contrary, as teaching artist Kaya explains, "I think especially girls of the ages we are working with have been stampeded, stampeded by boys . . . I think by finding their voice and playwriting as a vehicle for that, is getting back in touch with their impulses of who they are." And so the curriculum tells us, "Validate. Validate. Validate. Encourage. Encourage. Encourage. They are told in the facility, all day long. 'No. No. No.' 'Shut up, you can't do that.' 'Shut up.' 'You have to do this; you can't do that'. And in order to find their voice, you can't keep badgering it and cutting it down."

Maybe that's why Boal called theatre "a weapon of liberation."

Like a dressing room for trying on many selves, Our Place invites young women to experiment with new ways of being; to wrestle with their many desires, fears, anxieties, scars and dreams; to create an ensemble within the self, on the stage, and with others; to grow trust and courage in a community of support and recognition, even if the membranes of the space are thin, under surveillance, and routinely violated. That is, Our Place is a hybrid third space which invites many generations of women to collectively rewrite the scripts they have inherited and try on some new outfits. The question of freedom in such a context is, of course, thorny, thrilling, easy to romanticize and breathtaking. What does freedom mean for girls and women who have been "stampeded?" If we think for a moment about their lives before they entered the facility, and painfully, after, how constrained they are in these presumably "free" spaces.

When I worked at Bedford Hills Correctional Facility, a maximum security women's prison, I taught in the college program and then worked on a participatory evaluation of college in prison (Fine et al., 2003). Those of us who were free to leave boarded the train weekly with tears, rage, anger, respect, and a full body sense of having been in an existential hell. Outraged by the terms of confinement, lack of dignity, the time of commitment, the waste of lives and spirits, I would be stunned, often, when a woman would admit in class or an interview: "You know, I am a better mother in here than I was on the outside; this is the first time in years I have been free of male violence. I needed to get away for me and my children."

Those of us privileged enough to be outside of the system and looking in, not haunted by the real or remembered barbed wires of foster care, juvenile facilities, immigration centers, and prisons, may forget that many girls and women never feel free—on the streets, in the subways, at school, in the park, at home, in her own bedroom. It may be hard to appreciate why Sanaa would describe Meadow facility with nostalgia, where "the bread was soft and the JCOs were like mothers." It may be just too difficult to really think about her comparisons.

Girl Time is a text designed to pierce this anesthesia, to cut gently at the gauze of privilege that keeps some of us from knowing that freedom for most girls and women is fundamentally fraught, always compromised, routinely dangerous. The volume is animated by a relational and provocative courage that insists that readers contend with the embodied and gendered dialectics of freedom in confinement and oppression in presumably free spaces, insists that we awaken to the fact that for many girls and women freedom is a momentary pleasure, a soft wind on the cheek, a taste of cool water, soft bread, and a kind word. Sometimes these moments accumulate and paint a new sky; often the dark clouds retreat only to gather for a vengeful return.

Girl Time speaks through evocative justice for so many girls and women, across time, empire, and nation, enjoying an always marbled and chipped freedom, with swirls of desire, danger, terror, and laughter, within the most confined places.

Commitment

> In today's performance, the role of Commitment will be played
> by Diamond, Nia, Zaire, and an unnamed Correctional Officer.

It's a funny word, *commitment*. To be committed. Everyone in the performance of *Girl Time* is committed, in one way or another. Diamond tells us, "I am committed to the state. It's like 50 percent of me belongs to my mom and 50 percent of me belongs to the state. . . . I will be committed for eight years. But I am praying. I know I did bad and I'm going to do better."

Viola speaks of a set of relatively mundane, if painful, adolescent experiences that somehow accelerated, as if gasoline were poured all over them, tumbling her into commitment: "The first time I got locked up, they gave me probation and put me under house arrest. The second time I got real mad at my momma and didn't want to be in the same room with her and the same house. So I just left and I was gone for over 24 hours so I was charged as a runaway. Then I cut off my ankle bracelet as well, then I got locked up. . . . I got scared. I thought it would help them track me down. But I didn't know so I cut it off . . . [and then the third time?] It was again for my school work."

And you will remember that "Nia was in the hallway after the bell rang with a pass and an officer stopped to question why she was in the hallway . . . the officer started to search her . . . he found her lighter . . . at that point she was restrained, searched, handcuffed, and pepper sprayed when she tried to use her cell phone to call her mother. . . . 'So by the time I put the phone back in my pocket both of them [another guard] slammed me on the ground and threw me in handcuffs,' Nia was facing a charge of 'carrying a concealed weapon at school.'"

How do race, ethnicity, and class fast forward, for some young women, into [involuntary] commitment?

And then how do race, ethnicity, and class fast forward our work into other forms of commitment, as when Zaire explains that she plants seeds and watches them grow or Maisha tells us, "As a Black woman scholar I do not have the luxury to sit back, observe, and take notes without contributing to the community in some way, and nor would I want to because there is too much work to be done."

As I read and savored the scenes of *Girl Time*, I was flooded with images of commitments—stories worth telling, secrets that need to be buried, relationships in which women across generations could listen, hold, and "be with" each other. As these distinct and divergent forms of commitment huddled together in ensemble, a colorful collective of women dared to rewrite yesterday and tomorrow.

Readers of the text bear witness to this gift of *ensemble*: being taken seriously; being held; sharing fragile understandings of dignity, respect, and dissent. This *ensemble of commitments* is, perhaps, Winn's finest contribution to Teaching for Social Justice, modeling what it means to carve out spaces for and with young women who cultivate the courage to trust and speak, to stand tall and to step inside, for and with others, even when you are terrified:

"I said I wasn't going back period! I don't want to step foot [inside], I don't want to visit nobody. I mean they can call me, but I really don't want to go back. When I heard [my performance] is helping them or trying to help them I was like, 'okay I guess I can try to do this,' but I was really nervous when they said I was going back to Main!"

If *Girl Time* tells the story of an ensemble of commitments, it is also constituted by an *ensemble of stories of conviction* (another funny word) that reflect the strength to look oppression in the eye, to tell a bad story, to refuse a happy ending. Maisha Winn skillfully contests an overreliance on romantic educational ethnography, when she tells us "Girls wanted to create happy endings and who could blame them? . . . However, once in a while there were plays that challenged a 'happily ever after ending.'" Resisting the transcendent narrative, Winn forces us to confront the foreboding sky that was so familiar to Jada and the other young women.

You will remember the scene when Jada explained that she was sick of her home environment:

> "I like being here; it gives me something different to look
> forward to."

At that moment, Jada was stuck—without options, angry, desperate, and feeling betrayed. Trying to help, Maisha was "shocked at how illiterate [she] was at navigating 'the system' and how complicated it was to find a home for Jada—and her children." At the end of this wrenching story, there was a "dramatic exit" by Jada and her brother; a probation officer threatened them with arrest. Maisha Winn reflects, with what I can only imagine to be tears, on the page: "The very system we wanted girls to be liberated from had to step in and navigate an awkward confrontation, especially since we had the rest of the girls in the program bearing witness."

She continues: "I wondered if we were giving the false hope or selling a pipe dream that you really could be free. How much freedom does one have in a theatre program by day and a trap house by tonight? Other than one of the teachers taking Jada into her home. . . . There were not many options. While I do not think any of the teaching artists will ever get over what happened with Jada, I know that she forced all of us to think about our roles in the girls' lives and figure out ways to provide extended resources. We did theatre and arts well and provided a place for girls to perform their possibilities 'under a whole new sky'; Jada forced us to reconsider their realities as well."

Creating a space/stage/universe of second chances, youth advocacy, performance, an album of stories told in participatory literacy communities, Maisha Winn choreographs a world that is hard to bear and delicious—an ethnography of lives braided with pain and possibility. The text captures complex subjectivities of young women assaulted by racism, poverty, and violence against women—and surviving. These young women's stories are filled with laughter and friendship, fear and distrust. Winn gives us happy endings and frightening severed ties. She introduces us to a freedom in confined spaces, an ensemble of commitments, and a world that weighs heavily on young women, sometimes crushing them beyond support.

Girl Time captures an ethnography of the existential, the real, and the possible. Winn, like Boal, insists that there are no witnesses—there are no spectators. We are all "spectactors." With deep appreciation, I thank Maisha Winn for escorting us through the treacherous territory of girls' lives in America and for insisting that we act.

"Ghosts of the Past" Script

Characters

MONICA
ROBERT
DRE

SCENE 1. Lights up on Monica and Robert's house. The phone rings and Monica enters to answer.

MONICA: Hello? (*silence*) Hello?

DRE: What's up, baby girl. You sho' is hard to find. You hiding from me?

MONICA: What? Who is this?

DRE: Who you think this be?

MONICA: Dre? How you get this number? And why you calling me?

DRE: Look, we got some unfinished business. We need to make this bread like we used to. I been lookin' for you for a year. It's like after you got out, you just disappeared; and from the way you acting now, it seem like you ain't down no mo. I gave you some time to let the 12 stop watching you. Now it's time to get back on the grind.

MONICA: Look Dre, it has been awhile and my life is totally different now. I have a man that loves me and we are getting married. I can't go back to the block. That life ain't for me no more. Man I'm out!!

DRE: Oh really . . . so, what this man of yours do?

MONICA: He's an architect for a large firm. Why?

DRE: Well, I bet Mr. High Class don't know he rollin' with Lil Mon from the hood.

MONICA: What? Don't go there, Dre.

DRE: And I'm a even go so far as to bet you didn't tell him you did 10 years. Does that dude know he sleepin' with a convicted murderer?

MONICA: Nope, the past is the past and he ain't gone find out either.

DRE: Really, you think so? Lookie hear, lil girl. You playin' with my money and if Mr. High Class is what's in the way, then maybe I need to call him and let him know what's up. Your past just came callin' and it wants you back. So if I gotta salt your relationship, then a G gotta do what a G gotta do.

(DRE *hangs up.*)

MONICA: I can't tell Robert about my past. He wouldn't understand. He goes to parties and restaurants with food and drinks I couldn't even spell when we met. His parents live in a mansion. He ain't never set foot in da hood. But I love him and love my life with him. And now I'm about to lose all this. (*cries.*)

ROBERT: (*starts speaking off stage*) Baby, was that the caterer? (*He enters.*) Are they still trying to sell us those ugly flowers for the wedding? What's up? Baby, what's wrong?

MONICA: (*quietly*) Robert, we need to talk. I don't know how to tell you this, but . . .

ROBERT: Is this about the wedding? You didn't change your mind, did you?

MONICA: No, baby, I love you. But I didn't tell you some things about my past.

ROBERT: Oh, is that all? As long as you didn't kill nobody, I don't see what the problem is.

(*Big silence*)

MONICA: I did and served 10 years for it.

ROBERT: Girl stop playing (*laughing*).

MONICA: I grew up in the hood and all I knew was hustling.

(MONICA *and* ROBERT *freeze to indicate the telling of her story.*)

MONICA: And now you know. I'm sorry I didn't tell you.

ROBERT: What?! How could you not tell me all this before we got engaged and moved in together? I don't even know the person you're telling me about, which means I obviously don't know you!!

(ROBERT *leaves and slams the door behind him.* MONICA *follows him to the door.*)

MONICA: Robert, no, it's raining. Wait.

(MONICA *goes to pack her things. An hour passes. She goes to exit the front door and when she opens the door,* ROBERT *is standing there dripping wet with roses in his hands.*)

ROBERT: It was raining on these when I walked by them and I wanted to take them out the rain. Just like you. The past is over. So let's start again. Hi, my name is Robert and I'm the man you're going to marry.

(MONICA *starts crying and runs and jumps into his arms.*)

THE END

"Beauty and the Thug" Script

Characters

NARRATOR
ANALESE, a princess
PEABO, a thug

(NARRATOR enters and pulls up a chair like it's story time in a library)
NARRATOR: Gather around boys and girls, I want to tell you a story. A tale of love, adventure, and tragedy. *(Opens storybook and begins to read)* Once upon a time in a land far away called Koolash, where unicorns roamed free and flowers talked, there was a young princess named Analese.
(ANALESE enters and stands center stage)
NARRATOR: Now, Analese was depressed because she was to be married to an old, ugly, mean prince named Charles. Well, one day, as she was crying by the pond and talking to the flowers, a young man happened upon her.
(PEABO enters and listens to her talk to the flowers)
ANALESE: But I don't know why I have to marry him. I don't love him. He's short, with big front teeth and he's mean. He's always telling me what to do. What am I going to do? *(cries)*
PEABO: Yo. I'm saying, what you cryin' for, baby? You too fly for that.
ANALESE: *(breathless and shy)* Oh, hi.
PEABO: So, I'm sayin, lil mama, why you sittin over here lonely by yourself—talking to these flowers? Where yo man at?
ANALESE: Well my father is marrying me away to an awful man next week.
PEABO: Well, dang, Shawty. Why you sayin' it like that? You marryin him, you must love him.
ANALESE: Love him? I am a princess. It is my duty to marry who my father tells me to.

155

PEABO: I know who you are. I done seen you 'round the kingdom
     . . . struttin' your stuff, looking all good, wit ya tiara shining,
     bling-blinging in the sun. But, Shawty, if you don't wanna
     marry that dude then don't. You need to get wit a real playa. If
     you drop that zero, holla at ya boy.
(PEABO turns to leave.)
ANALESE: Wait . . . but I don't even know your name or where to
     find you.
PEABO: You'll see me when you are looking for me. Oh, and they
     call me Peabo.
(PEABO exits.)
NARRATOR: Analese watches Peabo leave and knows for sure
     that she loves him and must find a way to be with him. In the
     following days, she searches everywhere for him—high and low.
     One day, she is out riding her horse in the valley and sees Peabo
     sitting in a tree eating an apple.
ANALESE: Where have you been? I have been looking everywhere
     for you. You told me that if I went looking, I'd find you.
PEABO: Well, Shawty, you see me now. You gotta catch me. I be on
     the move.
ANALESE: Well, I told my father that I didn't want to marry Charles,
     that I wanted to be with you. So now, we can be together and get
     married and have lots of babies.
PEABO: Babies?! Wait. Hold up, Shawty. Where all this coming
     from? And m-m-m-married? Hold that down now, I don't even
     know you like that.
ANALESE: But you told me I was pretty and I thought you felt about
     me the same way I felt about you. It was love at first sight. Can't
     you feel how right this is?
PEABO: Naw, chick, I'm feeling how LEFT this is. Dang, I just
     wanted to kick it with you, maybe get a slice of pizza—pick
     some apples. But you trippin'. I might have to throw them
     deuces.
ANALESE: You don't have to throw anything. Why would you
     throw something at me?
PEABO: Naw, Shawty. You don't get it. I ain't wit all this yappin you
     doin—you tryin to get a brother hemmed up. You betta stick to
     talking to flowers. I'm outta here . . . Peace.
ANALESE: But wait, I love you. I gave up my crown for you.
PEABO: I don't love you and I ain't asked you to do that. Let's keep

it real. You don't know me. Is this how the girls in the palace get
   down? I'm cool. I don't want you. I'm out.
(PEABO exits.)
ANALESE: I don't understand . . . *(crying).*
NARRATOR: Once again the princess is left alone crying and talking
   to the flowers. The moral of the story, boys and girls . . . "You
   can bring a thug into a fairy tale, and he will still be a thug." The
   end.
THE END

"Ride or Die" Script

Characters

STARKIMA (STAR)
SMOKE
ASHLEY
COP 1 and COP 2 (small parts—only one line)

SCENE 1. Lights up on Smoke and Ashley in the bedroom of their house. Both are just waking up.

SMOKE: Where my breakfast at?

ASHLEY: I just woke up, like you.

SMOKE: *(slaps her)* Don't get smart with me *(grits his teeth)*. Girl, if you don't get up and cook my food, I . . . *(His phone rings. He looks at it and smiles)*

SMOKE: What's up, baby?

(ASHLEY looks at him and walks to the kitchen.)

SMOKE: You sold all that work for me?

STAR: You know I did.

SMOKE: You turned up them tricks for me?

STAR: Baby, I got all that money!

SMOKE: That's what's up! That's why you my down chick! Alright, I'll see you in 15 minutes at the hotel. Get dressed! Put on something sexy!

SCENE 2. In the Kitchen at Smoke's house.

(SMOKE walks into the kitchen and walks toward the door. ASHLEY puts his plate on the table.)

ASHLEY: *(looking disappointed that he is leaving)* Baby, breakfast is ready.

SMOKE: Got some business, Shawty. My house betta be clean when I get back!

(SMOKE leaves and slams the door.)

SCENE 3. At Star's hotel.

STAR: I can't believe Smoke tried me like a sucker duck! I been
    waiting on this busta for over an hour. He said he would be
    here in 15 minutes *(picks up her phone and dials)*. And he ain't
    answering his cell phone! *(starts looking through her phone)*. Where
    that number at he called me from the other day *(continues to look
    through phone)*. There it is!
(Phone rings)
ASHLEY: Hello.
STAR: Where Smoke at?
ASHLEY: Who is this?
STAR: This is his girl! Who is this?
ASHLEY: This is his wife! I believe you have the wrong Smoke
    sweetheart!
STAR: No, baby, I got the right Smoke and the right number!
(STAR hearing a knock, turns toward the door.)
STAR: Oh, honey, never mind. This is him now! *(STAR hangs up
    phone.)*
STAR: *(aloud to herself)* I got this! She won't be his wife for long!
*(STAR opens door and runs into Smoke's arms, crying hysterically, faking
    that she is upset.)*
Some woman just called and said she was your wife and all I am is
    a slut to you! She said that ya'll got kids and you just want five
    stacks out me. She said you going to leave me alone and I am
    nothing but your tramp slut!
SMOKE: Man! Baby, don't worry bout dis, I got that! Man! Dat girl
    ain't nothing, man, she just trying to make you mad girl—I love
    you!
STAR: Are you going to deal with her, baby?
SMOKE: I said I got it, man. *(storms out angrily.)*

SCENE 4. At Smoke and Ashley's house.

(SMOKE barges through the door.)
SMOKE: Who you thank you is?
ASHLEY: Who do I think I am, who is Star?
SMOKE: Who is Star? *(starts pushing her)* Who is Star? Sound like
    you know her. *(begins beating her)* Sound like you know her, after
    calling her.

ASHLEY: *(crying)* Calling her, she called me!

SMOKE: You a lie, she told me everything! Ima show you to lie!
    (begins beating her worse) That's my money maker, my ride or die
    chick. She do thangs you won't! Things you don't do!

ASHLEY: But she called here!

SMOKE: You a lie. Ween [We ain't] got to worry about that no more!
    I'll show you to mess with my money. *(SMOKE chokes her to death.)*

(SMOKE picks up the phone and calls STAR.)

SMOKE: We straight now!

STAR: What ya talking bout, baby?

SMOKE: Baby, I got rid of the problem!

STAR: That woman! I hope you ain't messing with her no more!

SMOKE: No, I ain't gon let nothin' mess with my money!

STAR: What you do? You cut her off?

SMOKE: Yea, she cut off . . . for good . . . I killed her!

STAR: What! *(screaming)* What!! You did What!

SMOKE: I did it for us and the money! She was talking bout turning
    us in to the feds.

STAR: Oh . . . *(long silence)*.

SMOKE: Well, I'm coming to pick you up, be ready!

SCENE 5. At Star's hotel room.

(SMOKE knocks on door.)

SMOKE: It's me baby.

STAR: Just a minute.

SMOKE: Hurry up and come open this door!

(COP 1 and COP 2 open the door, drag Smoke in, throw him on the ground.)

*(COP 1 reads SMOKE his rights, while SMOKE is delivering his next few
    lines. They talk at the same time.)*

SMOKE: *(talking to STAR)* Oh this how you gon play the game.

COP 1: You are under arrest for the murder of Ashley Turner.

SMOKE: You gon let this go down like this!

COP 1: You have the right to remain silent. Anything you say can
    and will be used against you in a court of law!

SMOKE: I thought you were my ride or die chick!

STAR: I was down for the ride, but I ain't down for the DIE!

THE END

Notes

Prologue

1. In order to preserve the voices of the Girl Time participants, I have let stand African American Vernacular English in their direct speech.

2. Adichie's talk, "The Danger of a Single Story," was retrieved from http://www.ted.com/talks/chimamanda_adichie_the_danger_of_a_single_story.html

3. This list is adapted from Belknap's (2001) *The Invisible Woman: Gender, Crime, and Justice*. Wadsworth Publishing, p. 168, and the Office of Juvenile Justice and Delinquency Prevention's (1998) *Guiding Principles for Promising Female Programming*, October, p. 2.

4. Kemba Smith was eventually granted clemency by President Bill Clinton in December 2000. See www.kembasmithfoundation.org

Act I

1. I added "her" to Boal's passage.

2. In this context, a "G" refers to a "gangsta" or someone who is smooth and even manipulative.

Act II

1. Federal, state, and local government agencies will sometimes contract out to private firms to manage their detention and correctional facilities for both adults and juveniles.

2. See Scot Brown (2005). *Fighting for US: Maulana Karenga, the US organization, and Black Cultural Nationalism*. New York: New York University Press.

3. In a discussion on August 25, 2010, Ginger was able to read through this passage and explained that she was in a place where she could name her experience as a form of White privilege. It was really powerful to revisit Ginger's interview transcript with her and for her to be able to name things that she did not have the language for initially.

Act IV

1. See NAACP's Legal Defense Fund's *Dismantling the School-to-Prison Pipeline*, retrieved from http://www.naacpldf.org/content/pdf/pipeline/Dismantling_the_School_to_Prison_Pipeline_BW_Version.pdf

2. See www.campaignforyouthjustice.org for testimonies of youth, their parents, and expert witnesses about youth being tried as adults. Campaign for social justice also has individual reports for each state that provide statistics for how many youth are being tried as adults, as well as their ethnicities.

References

Adichie, C. (2009). *The danger of a single story.* Retrieved from http://www.ted. com/talks/chimamanda_adichie_the_danger_of_a_single_story.html

Advancement Project. (2000, June). *Opportunities suspended: The devastating consequences of zero-tolerance and school discipline policies.* Cambridge, MA: Civil Rights Project, Harvard University. Retrieved from http://www.advancementproject. org/sites/default/files/publications/opsusp.pdf

Anyon, J. (1997). *Ghetto schooling: A political economy of urban educational reform.* New York: Teachers College Press.

Ayers, W. (1997). *A kind and just parent.* Boston: Beacon.

Belknap, J. (2001). *The invisible woman: Gender, crime, and justice.* Belmont, CA: Wadsworth.

Bell, J. (2000). Throwaway children: Conditions of confinement and incarceration. In V. Polokow (Ed.), *The public assault on American's children: Poverty, violence and juvenile injustice* (pp. 157–187). New York: Teachers College Press.

Bloom, B. E. (2003). *Gendered justice: Addressing female offenders.* Durham, NC: Carolina Academic Press.

Boal, A. (1979). *Theatre of the oppressed.* New York: Theatre Communications Group.

Boal, A. (2006). *The aesthetics of the oppressed.* London: Routledge.

Brown, A. L., & Brown, K. (2006). Tangling the knot, while loosening the strings: Examining the limits and possibilities of urban education for African American males. In J. Kincheloe, P. Anderson, K. Rose, D. Griffith, & K. Hayes (Eds.), *Urban education: A handbook* (pp. 460–470). Westport, CT: Praeger.

Brown, R. N. (2009). *Black girlhood celebration: Toward a hip-hop feminist pedagogy.* New York: Peter Lang.

Brown, S. (2005). *Fighting for US: Maulana Karenga, the US organization, and Black cultural nationalism.* New York: NYU Press.

Chesney-Lind, M. (1997). *The female offender: Girls, women, and crime.* Thousand Oaks, CA: Sage.

Chesney-Lind, M. (1999). Girls in jail. *Crime & Delinquency, 34*(2), 150–168.

Children's Defense Fund. (2007). *America's cradle to prison pipeline.* Retrieved from http://www.childrensdefense.org/site/PageServer?pagename=c2pp_report2007

Christensen, L. (2000). *Reading, writing, and rising up: Teaching about social justice and the power of the written word.* Milwaukee, WI: Rethinking Schools.

Corthron, K. (2002). *Breath, boom*. New York: Dramatists Play Service.

Covington, S. S., & Bloom, B. E. (2003). Gendered justice: Women in the criminal justices system. In B. E. Bloom (Ed.), *Gendered justice: Addressing female offenders* (pp. 3–23). Durham, NC: Carolina Academic Press.

Davis, A. Y. (2001). Foreword. In R. Fraden, *Imagining Medea: Rhodessa Jones and theater for incarcerated women* (pp. ix–xii). Chapel Hill: University of North Carolina Press.

Dohrn, B. (2000). Look out kid, it's something you did: The criminalization of children. In V. Polakow (Ed.), *The public assault on America's children: Poverty, violence, and juvenile injustice* (pp. 157–187). New York: Teachers College Press.

Duncan, G. A. (2000). Urban pedagogies and the celling of adolescents of color. *Social Justice, 27*(3), 29–42.

Engeström, Y. (1999). Activity theory and individual social transformation. In Y. Engeström, R. Miettinen, & R.-L. Punamäki (Eds.), *Perspectives on activity theory* (pp. 19–38). Cambridge, UK: Cambridge University Press.

Engeström, Y. (2001). Expansive learning at work: Toward an activity theoretical reconceptualization. *Journal of Education and Work, 14*(1), 133–157.

Evans-Winters, V. E. (2005). *Teaching black girls: Resiliency in urban classrooms*. New York: Peter Lang.

Fine, M., & McClelland, S. I. (2006). Sexuality education and desire: Still missing after all these years. *Harvard Educational Review, 76*(3), 297–338.

Fine, M., & Ruglis, J. (2009). Circuits and consequences of dispossession: The racialized realignment of the public sphere for U.S. youth. *Transforming Anthropology, 17*(1), 20–33.

Fine, M., Torre, M. E., Boodin, K., Bowen, I., Clark, J., Hylton, D., & Martinez, M. "Missy" Rivera, M., Roberts, R. A., Smart, P., & Upegui, D. (2003). Participatory action research within and beyond bars. In Camic, P., Rhodes, J. E., Yardley, L. (eds.), *Qualitative research in psychology: Expanding perspectives in methodology and design* (pp. 173–198). Washington, DC: American Psychological Association.

Fisher, M. T. (2003). Open mics and open minds: Spoken word poetry in African diaspora participatory literacy communities. *Harvard Educational Review, 73*(3), 362–389.

Fisher, M. T. (2004). The song is unfinished: The new literate and the literary and their institutions. *Written Communication, 21*(3), 290–312.

Fisher, M. T. (2005a). Literocracy: Liberating language and creating possibilities. *English Education, 37*(2), 92–95.

Fisher, M. T. (2005b). From the coffee house to the school house: The promise and potential of spoken word poetry in school contexts. *English Education, 37*(2), 115–131.

Fisher, M. T. (2006). Earning "dual degrees": Black bookstores as alternative knowledge spaces. *Anthropology and Education Quarterly, 37*(1), 83–99.

Fisher, M. T. (2007). *Writing in rhythm: Spoken word poetry in urban classrooms*. New York: Teachers College Press.

Fisher, M. T. (2008). Catching butterflies. *English Education, 40*(2), 94–100.

Fisher, M. T. (2009). *Black literate lives: Historical and contemporary perspectives*. New York: Routledge.

Fisher, M. T., Purcell, S. S., & May, R. (2009). Process, product, and playmaking. *English Education, 41*(4), 337–355.

Fishman, J., Lunsford, A., McGregor, B., & Otuteye, M. (2005). Performing writing, performing literacy. *College Composition and Communication, 57*(2), 224–252.

Fraden, R. (2001). *Imagining Medea: Rhodessa Jones and theater for incarcerated women.* Chapel Hill: University of North Carolina Press.

Freire, P. (1998). *Teachers as cultural workers: Letters to those who dare to teach.* Boulder, CO: Westview Press.

Freire, P. (2005). *Education for critical consciousness.* London: Continuum.

Gallagher, K. (2007). *Theatre of urban: Youth and schooling in dangerous times.* Toronto, Ontario, Canada: University of Toronto Press.

Gaunt, K. D. (2006). *The games black girls play: Learning the ropes from double-dutch to hip hop.* New York: NYU Press.

Ginwright, S. A. (2010). *Black youth rising: Activism and radical healing in urban America.* New York: Teachers College Press.

Green, K. (2010). *Youth speaking truth: The literacy practices of a youth-centered radio program.* Unpublished empirical paper, Emory University.

Greene, S. (2008). Introduction. In S. Greene (Ed.), *Literacy as a civil right: Reclaiming social justice in literacy teaching and learning* (pp. 1–25). New York: Peter Lang.

Gregory, A., Skiba, R. J., & Noguera, P. A. (2010). The achievement gap and discipline gap: Two sides of the same coin. *Educational Researcher, 39*(1), 59–68.

Gutiérrez, K. (2008). Language and literacies as civil rights. In S. Greene (Ed.), *Literacy as a civil right: Reclaiming social justice in literacy teaching and learning* (pp. 169–184). New York: Peter Lang.

Gutiérrez, K. D., Baquedano-López, P., & Tejeda, C. (1999). Rethinking diversity: Hybridity and hybrid language practices in the third space. *Mind, Culture, and Activity, 6*(4), 286–303.

Irvine, J. J. (1991). *Black students, school failure: Policies, practices, and prescriptions.* Westport, CT: Praeger.

Kelley, R. D. G. (1997). *Yo' mama's disfunktional! Fighting the culture wars in urban America.* Boston: Beacon.

Kerman, P. (2010). *Orange is the new black: My year in a women's prison.* New York: Spiegel & Grau.

Ladson-Billings, G. (2006). From the achievement gap to the education debt: Understanding achievement in U.S. schools [2006 presidential address to the American Educational Research Association]. *Educational Researcher, 35*(7), 3–12.

Lunsford, A. A., Moglen, H., & Slevin, J. (Eds.). (1990). *The right to literacy.* New York: Modern Language Association of America.

Madison, D. S. (2005). *Critical ethnography: Method, ethics, and performance.* Thousand Oaks, CA: Sage.

McGrew, K. (2007). *Education's prisoners: Schooling, the political economy, and the prison industrial complex.* New York: Peter Lang.

Meiners, E. R. (2007). *Right to be hostile: Schools, prisons, and the making of public enemies.* London: Routledge.

Nasir, N., & Hand, V. M. (2006). Exploring sociocultural perspectives on race, culture, and learning. *Review of Educational Research, 76*(4), 449–475.

NAACP Legal Defense and Educational Fund. (2005). *Dismantling the school-to-prison pipeline*. Retrieved from http://www.naacpldf.org/content/pdf/pipeline/Dismantling_the_School_to_Prison_Pipeline.pdf

Noguera, P. A. (2008). *The trouble with black boys: And other reflections on race, equity, and the future of public education*. San Francisco: Jossey-Bass.

Office of Juvenile Justice and Delinquency Prevention, (1998). *Guiding principles for promising female programming*. Washington, DC: Office of Juvenile Justice and Delinquency Prevention.

Paul, D. G. (2003). *Talkin' back: Raising and educating resilient Black girls*. Westport, CT: Praeger.

Peterson, C. L. (1995). *"Doers of the Word": African-American women speakers & writers in the North (1830–1880)*. Oxford, UK: Oxford University Press.

Pew Center on the States. (2008). *One in 100 behind bars in America 2008*. Washington, DC: Pew Charitable Trusts.

Plaut, S. (Ed.). (2009). *The right to literacy in secondary schools: Creating a culture of thinking*. New York: Teachers College Press.

Poe-Yamagata, E., & Jones, M. A. (2000). *And justice for some: Differential treatment of minority youth in the justice system*. Washington, DC: Building Blocks for Youth.

Polakow, V. (Ed.). (2000). *The public assault on America's children: Poverty, violence, and juvenile injustice*. New York: Teachers College Press.

Prothrow-Stith, D., & Spivak, H. R. (2006). *Sugar & spice and no longer nice: How we can stop girls' violence*. San Francisco: Jossey Bass.

Richie, B. (1996). *Compelled to crime: The gender entrapment of battered black women*. New York: Routledge.

Richie, B. (2005). Queering antiprison work: African American lesbians in the juvenile justice system. In J. Sudbury (Ed.), *Global lockdown: Race, gender, and the prison-industrial complex* (pp. 73–85). New York: Routledge.

Rose G. (1997). Performing inoperative community: The space and the resistance of some community projects. In K. Pile & M. Keith (Eds.), *Geographies of resistance* (pp. 184–202). London: Routledge.

Ruglis, J. (2010, April). *Circuits and consequences of dispossession*. Paper presented at the annual meeting of the American Educational Research Association, Denver, CO.

Simkins, S. B., Hirsch, A. E., Horvat, E. M, & Moss, M. B. (2004, Winter). The school to prison pipeline for girls: The role of physical and sexual abuse. *Children's Legal Rights Journal, 24*(4), 56–72.

Smith, A. D. (1993). *Fires in the mirror*. New York: Anchor Books.

Smith, K. (2005). Modern day slavery: Inside the prison-industrial complex. In J. Sudbury (Ed.), *Global lockdown: Race, gender, and the prison-industrial complex* (pp. 105–107). London: Routledge.

Stuart, R. (May, 1996). Kemba's nightmare. *Emerge Magazine*, pp. 28–48.

Sudbury, J. (2005). Introduction: Feminist critiques, transnational landscapes, abolitionist visions. In J. Sudbury (Ed.), *Global lockdown: Race, gender, and the prison-industrial complex* (pp. xi–xxviii). London: Routledge.

Vygotsky, L. S. (1978). *Mind in society: The development of higher psychological processes*. Cambridge, UK: Harvard University Press.

Ward, J. V. (2000). Raising resisters: The role of truth telling in the psychological development of African American girls. In L. Weiss & M. Fine (Eds.), *Construction sites: Excavating race, class, and gender among urban youths* (pp. 50–64). New York: Teachers College Press.

Winn, M. T. (2010a). Our side of the story: Moving incarcerated youth voices from margin to center. *Race, Ethnicity, and Education, 13*(3), 313–326.

Winn, M. T. (2010b). "Betwixt and between": Literacy, liminality, and the "celling" of Black girls. *Race, Ethnicity, and Education, 13*(4), 425–447.

Winn, M. T. (2011). Down for the ride but not the die. In V. Kinloch's (Ed.) *Urban Literacies: Critical Perspectives on Language, Learning, and Community* (pp. 125–141). New York: Teachers College Press.

Winn, M. T., & Behizadeh, N. (in press). The right to be literate: Literacy, education, and the school-to-prison pipeline. *Review of Research in Education.*

Winn, M. T., & Ubiles, J. R. (in press). Worthy witnessing: Collaborative research in urban classrooms. In A. Ball & C. Tyson (Eds.), *Studying diversity in teacher education.* Maryland: Rowman & Littlefield and American Educational Research Association.

Yang, W. K. (2009, September). Discipline or punish? Some suggestions for school policy and teacher practice. *Language Arts, 87*(1), 49–61.

Zahn, M. A., Hawkins, S. R., Chiancone, J., & Whitworth, A. (2008, October). *The girls study group—Charting the way to delinquency prevention for girls.* Washington, DC: Office of Juvenile Justice and Delinquency Prevention.

Index

Accountability, 36
Achievement gap, 111–112
Adichie, Chimamanda, 4, 161 n. 2
Advancement Project, 112
African American Vernacular English
    (AAVE), 27, 161 n. 1
African liberation, 52–53
After-school programs, 126
Air shifting (Green), 8–9
American Educational Research Association
    (AERA), 111
Anne (teaching artist), 12, 34, 37, 42–44, 45,
    55, 71, 90–91, 138–140
Anyon, J., 111
Authentic democracy, ix–x
Ayers, William, xii, 7

Baquedano-López, P., 6
Beatty, Warren, 86
"Beauty and the Thug" (play), 23, 25, 27,
    155–157 (script)
Bedford Hills Correctional Facility, 148
Behind the Cycle (working group), 71
Behizadeh, N., 110
Behn, Aphra, 42
Belknap, J., 4, 116, 161 n. 2
Bell, J., 5
Beyonce, 85–86
Black girlhood (Brown), 70
Black Nationalist ideologies, 103
Blocking, 27
Bloom, B. E., 73, 113, 114, 123
"Bluest Eye, The" (play), 76
Boal, A., 8, 19, 145, 147, 161 n. 1
Bonnie and Clyde (film), 86
Breakthrough (Somers), 109
Breath, Boom (Corthron), 42–43, 44
Brown, A. L., 117
Brown, K., 117
Brown, Ruth Nicole, 9, 70, 119, 124–126

Brown, Scot, 161 n. 2
Bullying, 50

California State Long Beach, 53
Candy (student artist), 2
Capacity, xv
Carrie Mae (teaching artist), 12, 16, 25–27,
    34, 47–49, 50, 88–89
Character development, 107–113
Chesney-Lind, M., 4, 113, 116
Children's Defense Fund, 110
Christensen, L., 22
Civil Rights Project, Harvard University,
    112
Class issues, 110
Clinton, Bill, 161 n. 4
Coalition building, 49, 123–126
Cognitive neuroscience research, xiv–xv, 36
Coleman, Bessie, 48
Colored Museum, The (Wolf), 93
Columbine High School (Colorado), 50
Committing, 142–143, 149–151
Corthron, Kia, 42–43
Covington, S. S., 73, 113, 123
Crack cocaine, 10–11
Cradle to prison pipeline, 110
Creole, 27
Cultural workers (Freire), 5, 34–35, 48–49.
    See also Teaching artists

Davis, A. Y., 126
Democracy, authentic, ix–x
Dialogue, importance of, xi
Diamond (student artist), 1
Disciplinary practices, 111–112
Discourse on personal responsibility (Fine
    & Rughs), 110
Dohrn, B., 113–115
Drug laws, 114
Drug mules, 10–11, 85–86

Dunaway, Faye, 86
Duncan, G. A., 5, 72, 110

Education debt (Ladson-Billings), 111
Education's prisoners (McGrew), 111
Emerge Magazine, 10–11
Engeström, Y., 6
Ensemble building, 18, 39–41, 48, 135,
        141–142, 150
Ethics, of teaching, xi
Evans-Winters, V. E., 119
Expulsion, 112
Eye contact, 22

Failing schools, 111
Feigned Courtesans, The (Behn), 42
Field, Sally, 47
Fine, Michelle, 4, 5, 18, 109, 110, 112, 116,
        117, 145
Fires in the Mirror (Smith), xiv
Fisher, M. T., 8, 27, 39, 41, 70, 124, 127, 133,
        148
Fishman, J., 18
Foster children, 115, 130–132
Fraden, R., 11, 18, 35, 86, 118, 123, 126–127
Freire, P., 5, 34

Gabrielle (student artist), 123, 127–130
Gallagher, K., 17
Games, theatre, 18, 22–23, 62–63
Games That Black Girls Play, The (Gaunt), 9
Gaunt, Kyra D., 9
Gender issues, 109, 113–120
German schools, ix
Ghetto schooling, 111
"Ghosts of the Past" (play), 23, 25, 27, 64,
        153–154 (script)
Gilligan, Carole, 119
Ginger (teaching artist), 12, 34, 57–62,
        116–117
Ginwright, S. A., 125–126
Girl power, 123–126
Girl Time
    character development and, 107–113
    commitment and, 142–143, 149–151
    described, 3
    double-dutch methodology and, 8–9
    evaluation of study of, 145–151
    formation of, 3
    freedom and, 146–149
    girl power and, 123–126

insider/outsider status and, 8–9
Kemba's nightmare and, 10–11, 85–86
    overview of, 11–13
participants in, 3–4
pedagogical practices in, 7, 12, 15–30
planting seeds of participation and,
        126–132
purpose of, 4
Regional Youth Detention Centers
        (RYDCs) and, 3–4, 6
school-to-prison pipeline and, 4, 12–13,
        51, 56, 60–61, 70–71, 107–120
self-discipline and, 4–5
student artists in. *See* Student artists
summer program, 9, 12, 17, 30, 67–120
supporting students outside of program,
        13, 121–144
teaching artists in. *See* Teaching artists
teaching philosophy of, 35
Green, K., 8–9
Greene, S., 70
Gregory, A., 111–112
Griffith-Joyner, Florence (Flo Jo), 45
Group homes, 131
Gutiérrez, K. D., 6, 22

"Hair Drama" (play), 93, 98, 127
Hand, V. M., 6
Harvard University, Civil Rights Project,
        112
Heath, Shirley Brice, xiii
"Hi, My Name Is Mariah" (play), 102
Hirsch, A. E., 4, 113, 116
Homophobia, 74
Hope and Redemption (film), 36–37
Horvat, E. M., 4, 113, 116

Ideological management (Meiners), 112
Imaging Medea (Fraden), 126
Insider/outsider status, 8–9
Irvine, J. J., 117
Isis (teaching artist), 12, 24, 34, 52–54, 58–59

Jada (student artist), 2, 65, 69, 91–97, 116,
        132, 145, 150–151
Janelle (student artist), 69, 101–105, 115,
        136, 140
Jardin (student artist), 15–19, 25–27
Jay-Z, 85–86
Jennifer (student artist), 2, 123, 130–132
Jill (student artist), 2

Jones, M. A., 117
Jones, Rhodessa, 11, 18–19, 104, 117–118, 124, 137
Jordan, Barbara, 48
Julienne (program assistant), 43–44
Julisa (teaching artist), 12, 34, 62–65
Juvenile Justice and Delinquency Prevention Act (1974), 114

Karenga, Maulana, 53
Kaya (teaching artist), 12, 20–29, 32–33, 35–41, 45, 49, 64, 67–68, 71, 93, 96, 98, 101–103, 122, 127, 132, 135, 137, 147
Kelley, R. D. G., 9
Kerman, Piper, 23
Kwanzaa, 53

Ladson-Billings, Gloria, 111
Layli (theatre stage manager), 105
Leon, Aya de, 101
Lesbian youth, 68, 74, 112
Lewis, Edmonia, 48
Liberating education, xii
Liminality (Madison), 5–6
Liquor use, 113
Lisa (student artist), 3, 69, 93, 97–100, 104, 134, 136, 137–140
Lunsford, A. A., 18, 70
Lupe (student artist), 15–19, 25–27

Madison, D. S., 3, 5–7, 17, 20, 22, 27, 143
May, R., 41
McClelland, S. I., 4, 116, 117
McGregor, B., 18
McGrew, K., 111
"Me and My Girlfriend" (song), 85–86
Medea Project Theater for Incarcerated Women (San Francisco County Jails), 11, 18–19, 104
Meiners, E. R., 72, 86, 110–112
Mindy (teaching artist), 12, 23–25, 33–34, 55–57
Moglen, H., 70
Momentary transcendences (Davis), 126
Mo'nique, 55
Moss, M. B., 4, 113, 116

NAACP Legal Defense and Educational Fund, 113
Name game, 22
Nasir, N., 6

Neoliberal movement, 5
Nia (student artist), 2, 68–69, 73–81, 104, 112–113, 134, 136
Noguera, P. A., 111–112, 117

Obligation, xv
Office of Juvenile Justice and Delinquency Prevention, 113, 114–115, 161 n. 3
Orange Is the New Black (Kerman), 23
Otuteye, M., 18
Our Place Theatre Company, 6, 20–21, 37, 42, 68–69, 147–148

Participatory literacy communities (PLCs), 8, 133, 134–135, 141–142
Pass the clap, 22
Paul, D. G., 118, 119
Pedagogy of Girl Time, 7, 12, 15–30, 41
    creating discourse of second chances, 136
    ensemble building, 18, 39–41, 48, 135, 141–142, 150
    multi-sited ethnographic fieldwork, 29–30
    performing, 134–135
    physical warm-ups, 18, 21–22, 62–63
    prewriting and writing, 18, 20–21, 25–27, 132–134
    staged readings, 23–25
    talk-backs, 23–25, 27–29, 118–119, 137–140
    theatre games, 18, 22–23, 62–63
    youth advocacy, 136
Pedagogy of questioning, xi
Performance ethnography, xiii, 6–7
Performance of possibilities (Madison), 3, 6–7
Performing inoperative community (Rose), 92
Permission, xv
Peterson, C. L., 6
Petulia (teaching artist), 12, 15–16, 25–27, 34, 49–52, 54
Pew Center for the States, 45–46, 117
Physical warm-ups, 18, 21–22, 62–63
Plaut, S., 70
Play, as first emancipation from situational constraints (Vygotsky), 18
Poetry, 101–105, 133, 138
Poe-Yamagata, E., 117
Polakow, V., 4
Positionality, 8–9
Positive people, 79–80
Power Writers (Bronx), 39, 70, 124

Prewriting, 18, 20–21, 25–27
Problem-solving strategies, 93
Prothrow-Stith, D., 4
Public enemies (Meiner), 86
Purcell, S. S., 41

Racial issues, 111–112, 116–120
Rae (student artist), 1, 132–133
Rape, 99–100, 116
Rearview mirror theory, 61
Regional Youth Detention Centers (RYDCs),
    3–4, 6, 18
Rehearse, as term, 18
Reynolds, Sean, 11, 104
Richie, B., 74, 114, 116, 119–120
"Ride or Die" (play), 85–88, 98–100, 127,
    158–160 (script)
Rose, G., 92
"Ruby Show, The" (play), 74–76
Rudolph, Wilma, 48
Ruglis, J., 5, 18, 109, 110, 112

Sanaa (student artist), 2, 68–69, 81–91,
    98–99, 114–115, 133–134, 138
School-to-prison pipeline, 4, 12–13, 51, 56,
    60–61, 70–71, 107–120
Self activity, xii
Self-discipline, importance of, 4–5
Self education, xii
Sexual abuse, 99–100, 116, 147
Silence, 118–119
Simkins, S. B., 4, 81, 113, 114, 116
Skiba, R. J., 111–112
Slevin, J., 70
Smith, Anna Deavere, xiv
Smith, Kemba, 10–11, 85–86, 114, 161 n. 4
Social justice
    promoting, 7
    teaching for, x–xi, 65
Sociocultural activity theory, xiii
SOLHOT (Saving Our Lives Hear Our
    Truths), 125
Somers, Suzanne, 109
Song writing, 97
Spanish, 27
Spectator (Boal), 8
Spivak, H. R., 4
Stagecoach Mary, 48
Staged readings, 23–25
Street theatre, 57–62
Student artists, 1–3, 5–6, 67–105
    Candy, 2

creating a discourse of second chances,
    136
Diamond, 1
ensemble building by, 135
Gabrielle, 123, 127–130
Jada, 2, 65, 69, 91–97, 116, 132, 145, 150–151
Janelle, 69, 101–105, 115, 136, 140
Jardin, 15–19, 25–27
Jennifer, 2, 123, 130–132
Jill, 2
learning from, 132–140
Lisa, 3, 69, 93, 97–100, 104, 134, 136,
    137–140
Lupe, 15–19, 25–27
Nia, 2, 68–69, 73–81, 104, 112–113, 134, 136
performing by, 134–135
Rae, 1, 132–133
Sanaa, 2, 68–69, 81–91, 98–99, 114–115,
    133–134, 138
talking back, 137–140
Taraji, 3
Tempest, 104
Tichina, 2, 134
Viola, 2, 115
writing by, 18, 20–21, 25–27, 132–134
youth advocacy and, 136
Sudbury, J., 45, 117
Suspension, 112
"Switch Around, The" (play), 121–122

Talk-backs, 23–25, 27–29, 68–69, 118–119,
    137–140
Taraji (student artist), 3
Teaching artists, 5–6, 31–65
    Anne, 12, 34, 37, 42–44, 45, 55, 71, 90–91,
        138–140
    Carrie Mae, 12, 16, 25–27, 34, 47–49, 50,
        88–89
    committing and, 142–143
    common denominators, 142
    ensemble as metaphor for learning
        community, 141–142
    Ginger, 12, 34, 57–62, 116–117
    interview process used by, 71–73
    Isis, 12, 24, 34, 52–54, 58–59
    Julisa, 12, 34, 62–65
    Kaya, 12, 20–29, 32–33, 35–41, 45, 49,
        67–68, 71, 93, 96, 98, 101–103, 122, 127,
        132, 135, 137, 147
    learning from, 140–143
    Mindy, 12, 23–25, 33–34, 55–57
    Petulia, 12, 15–16, 25–27, 34, 49–52, 54

recovery on the road, 142
relationships versus roles and, 140–141
Zaire, 12, 22, 28–29, 34, 44–47, 53, 67–69,
    87–88, 101, 103, 104, 115–116, 135,
    145, 146
Tejeda, C., 6
Tempest (student artist), 104
Theatre games, 18, 22–23, 62–63
Theatre of the Oppressed (TOP), 19
Thrown-away children (Bell), 5
Tichina (student artist), 2, 134
"To Bully or not to Bully" (play), 102–103
Totalitarian societies, ix
Truancy, 113, 115
"True Life" (play), 93
Tubman, Harriet, 48
Tupac, 85–86

Ubiles, J. R., 70, 124

Viola (student artist), 2, 115
Violence, 50, 114, 119–120

Voice, 20–21, 37–38, 64
"Voices Can Be Heard" (play), 17–18
Vygotsky, L. S., 18

Ward, J. V., 101, 119
Wells, Ida B., 48
Winn, Maisha T., 3, 22, 28, 65, 70, 72, 110,
    119, 124, 145–151
Wittow, Frank, 50
Wolf, George C., 93
Writing
    prewriting, 18, 20–21, 25–27
    by student writers, 132–134

Yang, W. K., 4, 112
Youth advocacy, 136

Zaire (teaching artist), 12, 22, 28–29, 34,
    44–47, 53, 67–69, 87–88, 101, 103, 104,
    115–116, 135, 145, 146
Zero-tolerance policies, 13, 60–61,
    114–115

About the Author

Maisha T. Winn (formerly Maisha T. Fisher) is a former public elementary school and high school teacher from Sacramento, California and has worked extensively with youth in urban schools and in out-of-school contexts throughout the United States. Her ethnography, *Writing in Rhythm: Spoken Word Poetry in Urban Classrooms* (Teachers College Press), follows the lives of student poets and their teachers from the Power Writers collective in the Bronx. Winn serves as an advisor to the documentary, "To Be Heard," about the Power Writers. She is also the author of an ethno-history of African American readers, writers, and speakers of the Black Arts Movement entitled *Black Literate Lives: Historical and Contemporary Perspectives* (Routledge). Additionally, her research has been published in numerous journals including *Harvard Educational Review*; *Race, Ethnicity, and Education*; *Anthropology and Education Quarterly*; *Research in the Teaching of English*, *Written Communication*, *The Journal of African American History*, and *English Education*. Currently Winn is an associate professor in Language, Literacy, and Culture in the Division of Educational Studies at Emory University.